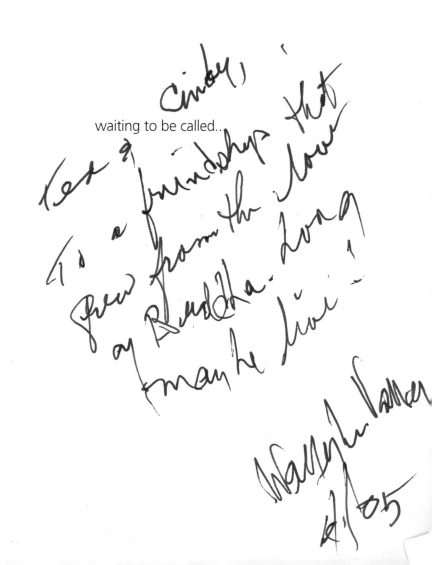

waiting to be called...

waiting to be called...

© 2005 by Wally LeValley

ISBN # 0-9676848-2-X

Published by Thunderbird Book Press

The author may be contacted at
wallylevalley@yahoo.com.

waiting
to be
called...

one man's reflections

Wally LeValley

ACKNOWLEDGMENTS

This book owes its existence to:

Janet Steinberg who planted the seed,
Ric Masten who made it sound easy,
Marikay LeValley who gave it shape and form,
Marnie Sperry for her awesome skills
both technical and editorial.
Lynn Archer and Jean Harnish for the final read,
and Bonny McGowan for her artistic talent
and untiring support.

Finally, to Illia Thompson and my classmates
who gave me reason to write
and a safe place to do it.

I thank you all.

Wally LeValley
Carmel Valley, California
2005

For my daughters,
Alyse and Evynn

TABLE OF CONTENTS

as I remember it...

Wally World

'What's in a name?' you asked. Join me as we trip through Wally World.

"Wallace Weber!" ...This from Grammy, screeching from the front porch when I was four or five. "Come home this minute."

Or, for variation on a theme, "*Wally* Weber!"...This from Mom, as in "Wally *Weber*, how many times do I have to tell you to wipe your feet before you come in the house? Were you born in a pig sty?" Mom loved clichés, but this one was lost on me. I mean, "pig" I knew, but what was a sty?

Or, "*Little* Wally"...This from every relative or neighbor who was taller than me, and that was darned near everybody. In my childhood I didn't mind being called Little Wally. It helped avoid confusion and sometimes embarrassment. My Dad was Big Wally, and he wore his title like King Tut.

It was not until a few years later, when I could see over the top of his head without standing on my tiptoes, and was still Little Wally, that I began to wish I had another name.

In the fifth grade I became Wally Walrus, named after a cartoon character popular at the time. I admit that this was during the pudgy period of my boyhood, but that didn't make Walrus any easier to live with. I thought I could take it, and I did until they put a dead fish in my lunchbox. After that, we moved to a nicer neighborhood.

If Walrus wasn't bad enough there was Wally, the sad-faced basset hound in the Sunday funnies, who drove his owners goofy by drooling on the sofa and peeing on the rug.

Or Wally, the guy on TV who lived next door and borrowed the lawnmower. He never returned it and made you feel guilty if you asked for it back.

And let me not forget Waldo J. Bunnyworth, the appellation given me by some yahoo from Texas in junior high. *Waldo* got lots of laughs at my expense. I was elated when the kid went back to Texas.

After high school I spent three years in the Marines where I was known as Webb. I figured that Webb wasn't too far from Weber, so that's what I told the guy at the recruitment office. It was time for a fresh start, I thought, time to grow up, become my own man. "Webb" worked okay in the Marines, but when I came home Webb didn't last long.

My folks couldn't buy "Webb." That's when Dad started calling me "W.W.," he being "W.B." (a much more masculine set of initials than mine). "W.W., did you mow the lawn both ways? It looks shabby. What did they teach you in the Marines?"

By my middle twenties I was stuck with "Wally" for life. W A L L Y   L E V A L L E Y. I mean, how sing-songy can you get? Some social deviant among my peer group went from Wally to Willy. From there it was a short hop to Lily. And from there to (can you see it coming?) Lily of the Valley. Jesus Christ! There was no escape.

But it's time to conclude this tour through Wally World with one more part about Big Wally. He loved his name. In his sixties he bought a cabin cruiser and christened it "Wally Ho." He had a gas powered golf cart that he would drive around town on his daily rounds. The license read: "Wally Ho." He bought a white, fringed, open-sided Fiat that he would decorate with flowers and drive in the Fourth of July parade. "Wally Ho" was painted on the trunk.

When he hit his eighties he wanted to give me the cart, the boat and the Fiat. I didn't take them, though. My reason was quite practical—I didn't have any place to keep them, and that's true. But you know, looking back on it now, I guess I knew I couldn't bear to change the name.

The Thing

I have never been as terrified as when Tubby McGraw and I saw *The Thing*. Thinking about it still gives me the chills. In case you don't remember it, *The Thing* was the most scary movie ever designed to turn an audience of boisterous, cocky 12-year olds into a puddle of fear. Some kids in the audience wet their pants. A couple had asthma attacks and their parents had to fetch them.

The scientists called The Thing *The Thing* because they did not know what else to call it. You never really got to see it, but you didn't need to. It was there.

The plot of the movie was simple. There was a small Army unit stationed somewhere where there was lots of snow and ice. One cold, miserable night there was a strange sound outside like something big sliding across the frozen surface. In the morning it looked like someone had skipped a gigantic, red Frisbee across a frosted lawn. Whatever it was, it was so hot when it came down it melted the ice and sank. Then it froze over.

The science and Army guys pooled their collective resources and decided that something weird was going on. Maybe a Russian secret aircraft had crashed. Or a flying saucer had come to earth, too fast. It was a mystery.

So the scientists cut through the ice and hauled up this big, oblong hunk of ice that seemed to have something in it. Whatever it was, they needed to keep it frozen and packed to be sent to the Army Research Center in Washington D.C. So they took the block of ice and put it in a storage shed for safekeeping.

A soldier was assigned to keep an eye on it through the night. This soldier is freezing his butt off out in this unheated shed. And, he is tired of looking at whatever it is inside the block. So, not being the swiftest private in the platoon, he throws a blanket over the block of ice.

Of course this poor guy is unaware that the blanket is electric and set on high. He can't see that, but we can, and there are some big inhales in the audience. Of course the blanket melts the ice—drip, drip, drip. Suddenly there is a dark shadow over the chair. The soldier looks up, horrified, and screams, and then it's lights out. They find him the next morning with all the blood drained out of his body.

The Thing is no dummy. It is sneaky and powerful and starts knocking people off one at a time. Then The Thing disappears for a while. A couple of days later the Army discovers a small vacant hut where The Thing has been busy raising small baby Things, all being fed from overhanging bottles of blood.

You find out, how I don't remember, that The Thing comes from another planet where the creatures that inhabit it are slowly dying out. To be saved, they must have something that can only be found in blood. This creature was assigned to find a planet where it could get all the blood it needed and take it back to the planet to save its people, or Things, from extinction.

I won't tell you the rest of the story in case you want to see it and scare the bejeebers out of yourself.

Let me end by giving you a tip on how to handle monsters of any kind, especially those who live in your closet or under your bed. Take off your shirt or jacket like Tubby and I did, pull the sleeve around so you can look out of it like a telescope, and when the monster gets too close, just squeeze the far end of the sleeve. If you can't see the monster, it can't see you. This is probably not a method you could patent, but it works. The Thing can't get you through a squeezed sleeve.

If it could, I wouldn't be here.

Where's the Sandlot?

When I was a kid, I loved to play baseball. There were no courts for basketball on Mercer Island. And football called for all kinds of equipment we didn't have. But with a ball and a bat you could play yearound.

With only one ball in our possession at any one time, if anybody hit one into the tall grass that grew thick in the outfield, the game was over, at least until one of us somehow got another ball. We got most of them from the left field bleachers in the old Rainier Stadium. The Seattle Rainiers of the old Pacific Coast League were our heroes. Management let us into the ballpark an hour before the games, and we earned a ball or sometimes two by shagging foul balls that ended up in the bleachers.

Most of the balls we earned this way had dings or smudges on them, but other than that they were visions in white. Of course, they didn't stay white for long. If you know Seattle, you know drizzle. To keep a ball from getting soggy, we would coat it with

Johnson's Floor Wax. Somebody had convinced us the waxed ball would last much longer in the elements than the unwaxed. Of course, he didn't tell us that when the waxed ball got wet, it turned brown, got slick as snail snot, and so heavy not one of us could make the throw from third to first on the fly.

When we weren't watching the Rainiers, we'd play with the bat in "workups" until it got too dark to see a brown ball coming at your head.

We were blessed with a flat lot across the road from our apartment complex. We never knew who owned the lot, but we knew he loved baseball. My dad said the owner could have sold that property for a bundle, but he'd rather see us playing baseball on it than see it developed into something ugly.

In the last few years, something has been happening to America's favorite game. The kids' levels, like Little League and Pony League, are being taken over by grownups. Drive by a ballpark where the kids are playing organized ball, and you'll see almost as many adults in the dugout as there are players on the field.

Adults schedule the games. They hold the meetings where decisions are made. They determine the line-ups and hire the umpires. They run the show. Don't get me wrong; many of the adults volunteer hundreds of hours during the season. But when are the kids left to figure out problems on their own?

And what happened to the camaraderie of base-ball? I never see the players at Little League games smile. This is serious business. It's stressful, getting coached and corrected in front of other people. The kids are doing their best to get the instructions straight, to not make themselves or their teams look bad. Play the way your coaches expect of you, and don't screw up!

Maybe I'm just jealous. I remember one time in the seventh grade when a rumor came 'round that a rich uncle of one of us was going to sponsor us as a team in a new city league for boys in our age group. We had never had the money to outfit a team and play in league ball. We were going to get new gloves, uniforms, bags and balls, even real bases to replace the odd-sized pieces of plywood that never would stay seated.

I confess. I was really getting excited about being on an organized team, even one with a coach telling me what to do. Then the whole thing evaporated, and we were back to "hit the bat" and "workups."

Maybe I'm too old to appreciate the benefits of organized baseball for kids. Maybe I'm missing out on all that "male bonding" I hear on talk shows. I suppose what I've written here will make me look like a disgruntled old-timer who's viewing his childhood through a tunnel of nostalgia. Baseball is a constant, yet changing game. I guess I should have changed along with it.

Autumn in New York

In 1961 I was stationed on Treasure Island awaiting discharge from the Marine Corps. I'd done my three years, and now I was a short-timer and got all the liberty I wanted.

I spent my free time in San Francisco's North Beach searching out the remnants of the fading culture of the beat generation. The beat scene had held a fascination for me that had begun a year earlier when I spent ten days on leave in Greenwich Village. From art galleries to coffee houses to dark bars, I wandered the Village, a youth full of curiosity and enthusiasm.

New York was good to me. I felt comfortable from the beginning. My first day in the Village, I found a room on McDougal Street, a street lined with aging three- and four-story townhouses built by the rich and famous before the turn of the century.

It was in the Village that I discovered poetry. It was everywhere: on walls, on windows, on every place where a poem could be posted. There were poetry readings night and day, usually free. I had never been to a poetry reading and my knowledge of things poetic was limited to the poems we read in high school. In the Village, much of the writing was protest poetry. It was dark and gloomy. I didn't understand it all, but I could feel it.

These poets weren't writing sonnets or villanelles. This was free verse, usually formless, shunning both rhyme and rhythm. This was poetry in the raw.

It wasn't just the poetry that peaked my interest. It was also the girls. They were visions in black. They were also distant and aloof. Some looked like zombies from "Night of the Living Dead." Still, I was intrigued and, I admit, a little scared. I had never seen girls like these before. A few of them were gorgeous.

I couldn't imagine having sex with one. What would we talk about after? I didn't write poetry, and I doubted if she'd be impressed by my recitation of "Casey at the Bat."

The main problem was that as much as I loved the Village, I still felt like an outsider, a farm boy in the big city. A clean-shaven square with a whitewall haircut. Besides that, it was becoming clear that I was too young to be a beatnik.

In New York I also spent a lot of time in Central Park with a girl I'd met at a party in the Village. She was not interested in the beat scene. She lived with her folks in Brooklyn and she came to Manhattan every day to a private school.

We took long walks in the park, and in my newfound enthusiasm for poetry, I read to her from *The White Pony*, an anthology of Chinese poetry that I had discovered in a secondhand bookstore.

Once we were on a teeter-totter on the edge of the park, near the street. She was perched on the high end of the board while I read to her from the low end. A city bus had stopped at the corner, waiting for the light to change. We paid little attention to it, until someone started yelling at us from the bus. We couldn't make out what he was saying. The passengers on our side of the bus had opened their windows and started to applaud. It took a minute to realize they were applauding us — a guy and a girl on a teeter totter reading poetry. As the light changed and the bus began to pull away, they cheered and waved goodbye. That moment has a special place in my memories of New York.

When my ten days' leave was up, goodbye wasn't easy. I didn't know what to say. We both knew we'd probably never see each other again. She wrote once, telling me how much she missed being together. I wrote back saying pretty much the same thing. I told myself that there were serious problems that prevented me from following through with this chance for romance. The hurdles were too high. For one thing, I had no money to travel. For another, there were five thousand miles between us and about to be more. I had been assigned a tour of duty in Okinawa.

But there was something else that stood in the way. She was on an academic path. She liked school and knew where she was going. I had no idea what I was going to do with the rest of my life. I had no goals and no ambition, and I knew it. When we were together in New York, we never talked about the future. We were living in the moment and that was enough.

Sometimes when I think about wandering around North Beach a year later, I wonder if I was really looking for the last remnants of the beat generation, or if I was looking for something I'd had, and lost. I don't know. But whenever Sinatra sings "Autumn in New York," I see a girl on a teeter totter in Central Park.

A Young Man in San Francisco

The house across the street was large and gray, and in the Queen Anne style. It had a cupola where, in my fantasy, an unpublished but gifted poet lived on cheese and cheap wine. The house itself was wondrous and magical, a perfect setting for a novel by one of the Brontes. It had an aura about it.

I would sit at my window and watch the fog come in from Ocean Beach, up past old Kezar Stadium, and on towards Buena Vista Park at the end of the Haight-Ashbury. When it got to Buena Vista Park atop a large round hill in the middle of the city, it would seep through the trees in broken patterns. It was a polite fog that always announced its arrival with little wisps of gray that gave you time to ready yourself for a shift in mood, as it crept around the Queen Anne, then to my house, before moving on downtown.

It really wasn't my house. It was an old rundown Victorian cut up into apartments. What I called my pad was two small rooms on the third floor, bathroom down the hall. It was tiny, Spartan, and perfectly suited to my needs. I was in my first year of graduate school at San Francisco State, and I was flat broke. By day I was a full-time student. By night, I took tourists to dinner in Chinatown and ran a later tour to the various night-clubs in North Beach. I'd get home from the tour about one in the morning, grab a few hours sleep, and then head off to class. Needless to say, both ends of the candle were burning brightly.

Between school and work I had no social life. My only friend was the bartender who lived next door. As for my sex life, for a young man living in the city where Tony Bennett left his heart, it was disappointing to say the least.

When I wasn't working or studying, I was lonely as hell. My salvation was that I was academically driven, or at least I had been the year before this one. Last year, if I had an assignment due, it was difficult if not impossible for anyone or anything to pull me away from the kitchen table I called my desk. I had set my goals at straight A's. Last year, following my rigid routine, I got them. But that was last year.

What friends I had made at S.F. State had all graduated and gone out into the world. I had already student-taught at a high school and didn't like it, so I decided to get a master's degree, which would allow me to teach at the college level. My problem was that I wasn't passionate about English literature, but didn't know what else to do.

One of my professors was fond of saying that loneliness is the human condition. "You'd better learn to live with it," he would caution. I can accept the fact that we are born alone and we die alone. I understand the poet who said, "We give birth astride the grave." But how to live life between birth and death? That was the question.

It was what the professor called the existential dilemma: how to impose meaning on your life, how to find your individual reason for living without being defined by outside sources like the church, political parties, or even families.

The existential hero is the person who determines his own path, develops his own moral code, and is willing to suffer the consequences of his choices. Loneliness becomes a certitude, something to count on like some people count on God.

The odds against such a person living a life of joy are overwhelming. If the self-defined moral code is too slack or too rigid, if the self-imposed reason for being is shaken, the loneliness that is always lurking in the background, can lead to despair, and from there to something to fill the empty void, often something like alcohol or drugs, or even suicide.

Most of my heroes were drunks. I didn't know that then. Then my heroes were merely flamboyant characters rejecting the norm. It was years later that I learned how they filled their void. Jack London, what a man! Dead at an early age of questionable causes. Ernest Hemingway, how I idolized him. Blew his brains out. Jack Kerouac, saying "yes, yes" to life as he pell-melled across America, before he died of alcoholism at his mother's house. Others come to mind: Tennessee

Williams, William Faulkner, Richard Brautigan, F. Scott Fitzgerald, all trying to maintain that existential stance in the face of oncoming despair. All in the end, finding it too difficult without booze or drugs.

These were my heroes. When I think about it, it's a wonder I'm still here.

It's a Question of Taste

A wise old Greek philosopher once cautioned his students in classical rhetoric thusly: "Stay away from questions of taste. They'll lead you where such discourse always ends, in a brawl. You will only discover that what you thought of as your 'good taste' is nonsense to someone else."

That warning from over 2,000 years ago still holds. In my case my wife says it's not an issue I should concern myself with because I don't have any, taste that is. For one thing, she disapproves of my wardrobe. I liked to wear blue and green together when such combinations marked you as a sartorial nerd. It was in "poor taste" they said. Now such color combinations are featured on the cover of "Vogue". My problem was that I was ahead of my time. It was the same with black and brown. "Oh, Jesus! You're not going out of the house like that, are you? Don't tell anyone where you live!"

Matters of taste change with the passing of time. What is grand style in matters of dress and manners to one generation may be abominable to another. The criteria of taste are not absolute. They're relative. So, as the Greek said, why argue?

Years ago in my early twenties, I shared an apartment in San Francisco with four other guys. I was a student at S.F. State by day, and a tire salesman for Sears at night. Don't laugh. Those tires paid the rent and kept creditors away from the door. (Truth is, I never had any creditors at the door because I never had any credit.) I'm proud to say that we kept that apartment for two years and never missed the rent.

It was a monument to bad taste. A triangular piece of plywood supported on bricks served as a dining room table. Matadors painted on black velvet adorned the walls. An old, smelly bearskin rug lay in front of the fireplace. It was missing both eyes and a front tooth, and it shed.

Nevertheless, the five of us kept things pretty well structured. Each of us had one night to cook plus some clean-up duties. It was there I learned to cook. Now they call it "heating". I may not know a lot about cooking but I know what I like, so I set out to develop a culinary repertoire.

First on my list of tongue-tingling delights was "Dinty Moore Beef Stew," a concoction of veggies (well cooked) and potatoes (well boiled) with little pieces of beef floating on the surface. We had "Dinty" every Thursday night with a few exceptions.

I also developed an uncanny knack for getting a Swanson's Chicken Pot Pie out of the tin and onto your plate without cracking the crust that held all the good stuff. Swanson's was a nice break from Dinty's. It took a time or two to get used to the slight taste of aluminum, but once you did, you were in for a real treat.

Another thing I learned in the kitchen while I was learning how to cook was that almost anything tastes better if it's pan-fried. Remember the electric frying pan? Saved my life. But the big discovery was that the best place in the house to eat was standing at the kitchen sink. If something slops, no problem. It also cuts down on all the walking back and forth that a cook endures. I've tried to convince my wife of this way of saving time and energy, but she insists we sit on chairs at the table at the same time.

My greatest culinary challenge was coming my way. Our next-door neighbor was suddenly called away on a business trip. He had just been to the market and bought a fresh chicken, which he would not be there to enjoy. So, he gave the chicken to us. He knew I was trying to stretch for new things on the menu. That bird was mainly muscle, and darn little fat. One roommate, a farm boy vrom Visalia, pronounced it a rooster. I didn't care. As Gertrude Stein said, " A chicken is a chicken,..." and so forth.

Since the chicken proved too big for the electric frying pan, my roommate and I decided to bake it. We were pretty sure that's what our mothers did to the turkeys on Thanksgiving, they baked them. Our reasoning was that a chicken is just a small turkey, so you stuff it. But stuff it with what?

Every day when we'd get home from class we'd discuss the perfect stuffing. Finally we ground up a box of graham crackers, added a little brandy, and stuffed the stuff into the bird. I told the other roomies that tonight they were getting something special. When I finished with the stuffing, I noticed that the chicken, which had been in the fridge for five days, didn't look so hot. There was a sort of greenish hue around the orifices. And it didn't smell like graham crackers. I called Gary, another roommate, into the kitchen. He took one look at what was going to be dinner and said, "Good God! It's gangrene!"

Crestfallen, we wrapped the corpse in a burial shroud, said our goodbyes, and slid him down the garbage chute. We heard him "thunk" into the garbage can two floors below.

It was four days before the garbage man would pick up. Even though he was long dead, this chicken made his presence known. One middle-aged man from downstairs was snooping around looking for the source of the strange smell. When he reached our apartment, Gary and I were fixing the carpet in the hallway. He walked up to us and said, "You boys know anything about that terrible smell?"

Gary looked over at me with an absolutely straight face and said, "What smell?" At which point the guy walked off mumbling under his breath. We went into the apartment, closed the door, turned on the stereo, and damn near died laughing.

That was my first and last attempt to cook a chicken. I made it up to my roomies by serving one of their favorite dishes: tuna melts on sesame buns. When it comes to taste, I know my limitations.

Juan

"Wallacito, you have to learn to live with spots."
We were looking at my brand new living room rug.
It had a dark stain on it about the size of a manhole
cover. During the night, either Juan or Anna, his travel-
ing companion, had knocked over a bottle of baby oil.
By morning it had spread itself into a perfect circle on
my new rug.

Needless to say, I was unhappy. As I began to admon-
ish my houseguests, Juan rolled over and snuggled up to
Anna, who wasn't awake yet. As suddenly as it had
started, my righteous anger began to subside. It was
hard to stay mad at Juan.

"Wallacito, you've got to learn to live with spots."
Juan's simple advice still echoes through my mind.
I knew what he meant. He wasn't talking about the
stain on the carpet. He was talking about the way I
lived my life, bluffing my way through, alone, with my
dog and an account at Grapevine Liquors.

Before he was Juan, he was Jack Lautz, a successful

Los Angeles stockbroker. He had all the toys of success: the perfect car, the great apartment, and the beautiful wife. Then one day he came home from work and his wife was gone. So was the car. There was no note of goodbye. She was simply gone. He knew she'd been unhappy about the long hours he spent at work, but he thought that would pass. They were certainly doing well financially. What else did she need?

After she left, he went off the deep end. He locked himself in his apartment for almost a month. When the landlord and a sheriff's deputy arrived, they had to pry the door open to get in. There were piles of trash and garbage all dumped in the middle of the living room. They found Juan hiding in a back closet.

After being questioned by the deputy and yelled at by the landlord, the sheriff arrested him and off they went to jail. The upshot of the whole thing was that Juan was sent to Agnew State Hospital for a complete psychological examination. He had mentioned suicide to the deputy, and a judge thought a mental hospital would be the safest place to put him, at least until he could come to grips with his situation.

When he showed up in Carmel Valley, he was driving the requisite vehicle of the sixties: an early vintage VW van with a wooden roof of his own design. It looked like a little shepherd's hut with wheels. The windshield was framed with feathers he'd collected along the road. The dashboard was covered with something like peat moss. On this moss were several candles and some sticks of incense. Added to this was the overwhelming smell of patchouli oil, which was unmistakable.

Juan was thirty years old and a little over five feet ten inches on a well-built frame. He could knock down a six-pack more than once during a day and never put on a pound. His face was a little narrow for his build, giving him a hint of some Middle Eastern influence a few generations back. With his sand-colored hair styled by the wind, he attracted ladies with relative ease.

Not long after his arrival at Agnew, he met Anna, a sweet, rather quiet nineteen-year-old from Monterey. She had been seduced, knocked up, and abandoned by her former husband and suffered a total collapse. In their group therapy sessions Juan and Anna had become friends, watching out for each other and trying to stay straight enough to earn their release from the hospital. Neither of them quite wanted to remember all the rules the rest of us lived by.

After their release, they settled into a tiny place in Carmel. As time passed, Carmel cops came to know Juan and not only tolerated his sometimes bizarre behavior, but took an interest in his and Anna's well being. Juan had some sort of charm you couldn't deny, and couldn't define either.

It was my first year of teaching at Carmel High School, and I had a feeling that as a middleclass school teacher I shouldn't be hanging around with a strange character who drove into the middle of the Carmel City Park and set out his marijuana plants for what he told the cops was a "sun bath".

Juan was not what was classically called a hippie. He kept his hair short and avoided costumes. He was not even a member of what was then called the counter culture. He was free to be himself. I was envious. I felt bound by the unspoken expectations of what Carmel and its high school expected me to be.

That winter I wrecked my car on a drunk and stormy night. Thank God, no one was with me, and no one got hurt except the car, which was totaled. Somehow I got it home by the good graces of the sheriff's department. The next morning when I saw the car I was overcome by guilt and remorse, which finally worked its way to shame.

When Juan saw the car he said, "Wallacito, what happened?" When I told him the story he was silent a moment. Then he said, "They cannot take your life." I started to protest what seemed like a shallow response to my despair. I was really feeling sorry for myself and I was writing terrible scenarios for my future. Mainly, I would get fired when they found out I was drunk.

Then Juan said, "How serious is this? In the long span of your life, how important do you want it to be? That is a question worth answering."

Nothing came of my fearsome scenarios. I didn't get fired. In fact, I taught there for seventeen years. I still work there when they call me. Anna went on to have a beautiful son who has recently graduated from college, much to his mother's delight. She's now living in Monterey.

Juan hung around the Valley for about a year, until he met a woman and moved to a little town in Northern California where he got a job with an irrigation company working outdoors, which is where he wanted to be. I visited him once, met Juanna and their three boys who all looked like their dad. He had everything he'd been looking for.

I still have an aversion to spots, but when one comes along I ask myself, "How serious is it?"
A guy named Juan taught me that.

remnants...

Thank You, Sergeant Schmidt

I can't tell a joke. After so many failures I've trained myself to forget punch lines so I won't be tempted, not even by one of those rare jokes that leave me wiping my eyes from laughing. If I tried to tell the same joke, I'd screw it up. So I stay away from jokes, but I appreciate a sense of humor.

Bob Hope could be funny. He was one of the world's great comedians, yet his comic routine was the same everywhere he went. He'd deliver a monologue that was full of jokes scripted by professional writers. The jokes made people laugh in a comfortable way. You always knew Hope wouldn't take you too far out there. You always had control; it was safe humor.

I never saw Hope ad lib or shoot from the hip. I'm not trying to sully Mr. Hope's reputation. I loved his movies when I was a kid. But as an adult, he seldom made me laugh. He was funny, but not witty.

When I think of wit, I see Robin Williams on stage at Carnegie Hall. He's out there on a limb, taking risks no one else does. The quickness of his wit, and its effect on the audience, is awesome to behold. A tour de force in free association, and courage!

What is wit? We all recognize it when we see it, but just how it works is difficult to define. Webster gets part of it. He says wit has to do with giving people a new or often more irreverent way of seeing things. It shows, in a humorous way how two seemingly unrelated situations are actually quite similar.

Poets work something like comics do. They flash into the heart of things. They show us what was really there that we didn't see. For example, you have a junk drawer somewhere in your house, usually in the kitchen. It's full of bits and pieces, some broken parts, stuff you'll never use but can't throw out. I've got such a drawer. I open it probably two or three times a day, looking for something with which to fix something else.

One day a poet will be searching for something in his junk drawer, and in what you might call a flash of insight, the junk drawer becomes a metaphor for mankind in a muddle. He sees the alienation of us all, one from another, or the drawer becomes a symbol of our cluttered lives.

My best friend once asked me where I got my wit. I told him I had no idea, I'd never considered myself to be "witty". My father was a great joke teller, but he had little wit, a term which has lost much of its original meaning. I have a feeling that what wit I have, developed initially as a defense mechanism of sorts. In my late teens I was a depressed, unhappy kid, and I was very sarcastic. It helped me keep people from getting too close. I was good at the put-down. Most sarcastic people think they see the real truth of a situation, and are more than willing to share with you, at your expense, the wisdom of their discovery.

The Marines made it possible for me to give up a lot of my sarcasm. There was still some of it left over when I got out of the Corps. It took years to give up what I had depended on for so long. Although I didn't know it at the time, something good had come out of those three years in the service. Where I once would have responded with sarcasm, I began to respond with humor. I had grown to like myself.

I was a cocky, manic-depressive adolescent before the Corps. But as I've said elsewhere, there is no one on the planet less impressed by your sarcasm than a Marine Corps drill instructor. Sergeant Schmidt, wherever you are, I owe you more than you'll ever know.

Assaulting the Olfactory Canal

I was picking my way across the levees that separated the paddies. I was trying hard not to step into the
water. It was getting dark. Rats were scurrying along
the pathways searching for anything edible. They were
the size of small cats. I gave them a wide berth. I was
more afraid of them than they were of me.

I was coming home from the village where I had
just left a couple of buddies at a beer joint. I wanted to
get back to the base by going across the paddies before
it got too dark. Otherwise, I'd have to take the road
back, which would have been a two-mile trek in the
dark.

Luckily the moon was almost full, and it reflected
off the ponds. I stopped for a moment in the fading
pink light, looking back at the village. I could still see
the light from Mr. Kim's where I left my two friends.

Mr. Kim's was a small bar with a packed earth floor.
Mr. Kim, the owner, had a battery-operated phonograph
and three albums, one of which was Ahmad Jamal, an

innovative pianist in the late fifties and early sixties.
He had an unmistakable touch and I could hear his
piano drifting out of the village.

As I was standing there on the levee, a slight breeze
came up from a different direction. With it came the
smell of something strange, something awful. As the
breeze picked up, so did the smell. There was no
escaping it in the near dark on a mud levee. My God,
what could smell that bad? Whatever it was, it brought
an abrupt end to my moonlight reverie.

The smell was getting worse. It was rank and
rancid. Had the rats turned up something putrid? A
dead animal, or a dead person? It is hard to compare
the smell to anything you might know. My nostrils had
never encountered anything like this. They were send-
ing puzzled messages to my brain. It was a sharp smell
like Limburger, but at the same time hot, fiery like
cheap mescal. It stuck in your nose like sour vomit.

A few days later I was relating this incident to a G.I.
who'd been in Korea for three years. After my retelling,
he said the odor was undoubtedly kim chee, a staple in
the diet of people in rural areas. He said in the cities the
people loved their kim chee but weren't allowed to
make their own. It was easy to see why.

Kim chee is a combination of rotting vegetables
and spice, all packed into an enormous ceramic jug
and stored under the house in a kind of root cellar.
As it ages, it begins to ferment. By the time the jug
is brought into the house, it contains a lot of gas.
Sometimes the gas is so strong, not to mention
offensive, it will blow the lid off the jug.

That is what I had smelled. Some family had opened one of the jugs. And the breeze had done the rest.

As far as the nose goes, that was an evening I will never forget. I never got used to the smell of kim chee, but who was I, an American, raised on the smell of Mel's Drive-Ins and backyard barbeques? Who was I to be condemning another country's olfactory delight? I was told a Korean could use kim chee to brighten any dish. I don't doubt it.

Kipling said, "East is East and West is West, and never the twain shall meet". Few people know this, but he wrote that line immediately after his first encounter with kim chee. Really.

What the Hell is Aubergine?

Years ago I loved baby blue. My carpet was baby blue. So was my '58 Chevy and half my wardrobe. It was a soft, unobtrusive color that lightened my load, lifted my spirits, and made me cool. Then the Chronicle came out with a story that alleged Baby Blue to be the favorite color of Liberace. I knew the article was based on poor research and highly suspect, but it took the joy out of baby blue.

Since then I've really tried to pay attention to colors — what's in and what's out. But now I find that since my blue days, someone has screwed up the color chart.

For example, what color is puce? Puce was not in my crayola box. Neither was okra. In my day okra was like zucchini, you fed it to the dog under the table. Or eggplant, which parents have used for centuries to torture their offspring.

And pepper, which, I'm told, is some shade of red (remember red?) Not to be confused with tangerine, which is another color altogether. pepper has always been black when they put it on your salad. Let's not forget pumpkin. Pumpkin I can see. Having sneaked and eaten two and a half pumpkin pies at Grandma's one Thanksgiving when I was seven, and having a gastronomical reaction that would rival Vesuvius, I can no longer abide pumpkin.

As a man I find it both difficult and embarrassing to go into a men's store and be unable to communicate with the sales people.

This year's "in" color for men is aubergine.

A Short History of Hats

Anthropologists agree that no other item of man's apparel is so much a product of sheer necessity as the hat. On the cave walls of Lascaux, recently restored, there is an entire section dedicated to hats.

These ancient head covers served two important functions: 1) They kept the ears close to the head in sub-zero temperatures. The formula for survival was simple: no hat, no ears. 2) They allowed the blood in the brain to rise two degrees Fahrenheit, thus promoting a small but significant enlargement of the cerebral cortex, which, in turn, boosted the average IQ from 56 to 62. This boost of 6 points in intelligence quotient ultimately led to the invention of the wheel, which, down through the ages, reached its culmination in the Volkswagen. All this from hats.

Over the thousands of years since Lascaux was first occupied, hats developed from clumsy and often smelly head gear to something even more necessary for survival: the helmet. (Our space in this writing is too limited for a full discussion of the helmet in history, but for readers fascinated by the subject, see Professor J. G. Muddlesome's *The Mesopotamian Headdress*, and Dr. Ivan Doogle's three volume *Headgear for Helots*.)

As man evolved and gained confidence in his chances of reaching 35, the hat evolved from a simple product of necessity to a symbol of where the individual fit into the great chain of being. The social function of the hat had arrived. From the flamboyant chapeaux of Versailles, to the floppy fedoras of America in the 30's and 40's, any man without a hat (or cap, in some circles) was suspect. At best, he was considered anti-social and outside the social norm. Most men yielded to the peer pressure, and donned a hat.

In the 1960's, man was finally liberated by the hippies who wore all sorts of things on their heads. Many eschewed the hat altogether and let their hair grow long. Sociologists said that without the hats, the hippies had an uncanny likeness to their Neanderthal forefathers. There were other similarities between the two groups, but funds were never available for a thorough study of this anthropological connection.

Finally we have come to the most basic and func-tional of all hats, the baseball cap. Everyone wears one everywhere, indoors or outdoors, day or night, it doesn't matter. Young women, for example, cannot drive a sports car without a baseball cap, preferably with a little tuft of hair sticking out the back. In fact, without her cap, she'd have to leave the S.U.V. in the garage.

The modern cowboy has also discovered the ball cap. There he stands, Tony Lama boots, Wrangler jeans, Calvin Klein long-sleeved shirt with mother of pearl buttons, and on his head...not a Stetson, but the cap, often advertising some service or product on the front, something like "Hacienda Hay & Feed," or "Peterbilt Trucks," or, more recently, "Viagra."

You can tell when a society has reached the zenith of its cultural evolution. The first thing it does is drop the hat. The Mayans, for example, ceased wearing hats as soon as they perfected their astronomy. They had found their place in the universe. Like the Mayans, the Anasazi Indians from the American Southwest stopped wearing hats when they brought cliff dwelling architecture to perfection.

"Where are those cultures now?" you ask. They've evolved to a higher place in the cosmic scheme of things. They don't need hats.

I didn't mean to ignore women in this brief discussion. Women, after going for a few thousand years of often vitriolic debates over function vs. fashion, were almost liberated from hats by the Kennedy Administration. Jackie had a start on it. Unfortunately, she wasn't in the White House long enough to see it through.

Actually, when you think about it, Jackie was premature in her efforts. There's still some doubt we've reached the zenith of our culture.

A Briar Patch is What You Make It
(to be read aloud)

One of the craziest sights I ever saw was a flying rabbit. Well, maybe not flying exactly, but airborne for sure. It went like this:

Brer Rabbit sat on the low end of the seesaw. He was on the low end cause there wasn't anybody on the high end. When I saw him I hollered, "Hey, Brer Rabbit, what you doin'?" "Just sittin' here," he said, "restin'." He was taking a break from Brer Fox who had many times invited him home to dinner, but since Brer Rabbit was no dummy and didn't want to *be* dinner, he kept declining the invitation, which infuriated Brer Fox.

Brer Rabbit and I were jest sittin' there jawing away when Brer Bear came lumbering out of the woods. That put Brer Rabbit on his guard, but he never moved from the seesaw. As long as there were a few feet between him and Brer Bear, Brer Rabbit could be as cool as a mint julep. It was no secret that Brer Bear was a little slow, just one honey pot short in the pantry, people said.

Brer Bear gave his usual greeting to Brer Rabbit:

"Dah, I'm gonna knock yo' head clean off." Then he started to swing his big club around over his head. Still, Brer Rabbit didn't move. Suddenly Brer Bear brought the huge head of the club down on the high side of the seesaw where nobody was sitting.

Brer Rabbit shot up into the air like a cork coming out of a bad bottle of sarsaparilla. At this point Brer Fox leapt out of the bushes with a big fisherman's net (where he got it only he knows). "Grab the other end, idgit!" That's what he always called Brer Bear: Idgit.

So in a twinkling Brer Fox had the net all ready for when Brer Rabbit came back down. And "kaphump!" Brer Rabbit came down right in the middle of the net. Before he knew it, he was stuck so far down in this net, not even his ears stuck out.

"I gotcha, I gotcha, I gotcha!" cackled Brer Fox. "Now we can finally have that dinner together."

"What about me?" asked Brer Bear. "I done all the work."

"But it was my plan, idgit!"

While they were jawing with each other, Brer Rabbit was searching for some way out of the net, but there wasn't one. He was sweating like a stuck duck, and he was thinking he was in a bad way this time. When they finished their argument over who would get the choicest piece of Brer Rabbit once he was fricasseed, Brer Fox picked up the net and threw it over his shoulder. "Come on, idgit," he said, "I'm hungry."

Now this next part is borrowed from Uncle Remus, and I hope I tell it right.

As they were passing the briar patch, Brer Rabbit started to howl like a coyote in heat. "Yowll, ool yaool

yaool. They going to throw me in the briar patch and kill me slow. Not the briar patch! No! Any way but that! Oh, please!"

Well, that "please" was just what Brer Fox needed to change his mind. It added something special to Brer Rabbit's coming demise. Then Brer Fox says to Brer Bear, "Grab him by the ears and throw him clear out in the middle of this briar patch. All the trouble he caused me, I wish there was something worse for him!"

So Brer Bear reaches into the net but he can't find the ears until Brer Rabbit hands them to him. At that point, Brer Bear twirls Brer Rabbit three times over his head, and launches him smack in the middle of the nastiest looking briar patch you ever did see.

When Brer Rabbit hit the horrible stickers he screamed and whooped and hollered like he was dying a slow, painful death. Brer Fox broke into a little jig. "I got 'im, I got 'im, I got 'im!" he said over and over again.

After a while the terrible sounds from the briar patch stopped. It was perfectly quiet. Brer Fox suddenly felt a little sad. Then he felt real sad. The game was over. Brer Rabbit was gone. Brer Bear sat down on a log and hung his head. "Things'll never be the same," he said. That afternoon changed them both.

As for Brer Rabbit, he was long gone from the briar patch. He had been born in the briar patch and knew every briar in it. He knew the secret trails only the rabbits knew. There wasn't a scratch on him, but he knew the game was over. Now he'd have to grow up and find a new place.

Brer Rabbit survived into old age. He made his living as a carrot farmer. Raised the best carrots you ever saw. Brer Bear got a job as bouncer at the local Moose Hall. He had to wear a tie. So far he hasn't knocked anybody's head clean off. As for Brer Fox, nobody around here knew what happened to him for quite a while. Last we heard he was selling time-shares in Hawaii.

I"ll Never Have a Dog Named Spot

When Lady Macbeth cried out, "Out, out damned spot!" I don't know whether she was chasing the dog, struggling with a wine stain, or agonizing over a liver spot. It doesn't matter. What I've always admired was the economy of her command.

One of the most memorable scenes in the play is about spots. The Bard knew his stuff. The subject was so important to Lady Macbeth, it kept her up nights. I have always sympathized with that woman, for spots, in all their forms as smudges, smears, and stains, drive me crazy. Right now I have spots on my lawn, brown patches that will not go away. My nurseryman says that they are some sort of fungus. If so, they are a hardy lot. They've been sprayed, aerated, and mightily cursed. They may shift around from time to time, but they are loyal to my lawn. So far, not one has yielded to my threats.

My dog has another theory about brown spots. What she can't understand is how other members of her species get inside the yard. After all, it is fenced and it is her territory. Whenever she sees a new blemish on the green, she looks perplexed, depressed, even violated. And then she pees on it.

My counselor says that I see the spots as faults, blemishes on my soul. He says that when I have a healthy respect for myself, the spots will go away, or that at least I will not care about them anymore. He thinks that I see them as evidence that I am too stupid to make grass grow. He may be right. So I asked him if he could not minister to a lawn diseased. He gave me a strange look, and put me down for another appointment.

I have a friend named Juan who never sees the spots at all. He can be standing in the middle of a brown patch the size of a launching pad and see only the green at the fringes. I've never understood him. He once said to me, "Wallacito, you've got to learn to live with spots." Then he smiled benignly, like a holy man with a secret.

I think he was onto something deep. Unfortunately, he was only on weekend leave and had to report back to the ward before they found him missing. Anyway, if Lady Macbeth had heeded Juan's advice, she could have stopped stalking halls.

So could I. It's been keeping my wife up nights.

Aunt Bettie

I can see her dancing now. Not exactly dancing.
More like stoutly hopping to the beat of Al Green's
version of "Pretty Woman" or "Operator" by Manhattan
Transfer. With her coal black hair and summer tan she
could just as well have been at a rain dance in Idaho
with Great Grandma, who was known to the family as
"The Squaw." Great Grandma was a blackfoot Indian,
and before she died at an old age, she let it be known
that Bettie was part Indian "with a little Scotch thrown
in to liven things up." Her words were prophetic. If
there's one thing Bettie Norwood O'Neal knew, it was
how to liven things up.

Right now she was having a great time dancing in
her living room with the rug rolled up. She had on her
white go-go boots (this was the seventies), a loose red
skirt, and a black puffy blouse. She was still wearing her
hair in a "chopped bob," just as she had in college. In
fact, she still looked like her yearbook picture, especially
in the photo of her all-girl cadet auxiliary team.

The Second World War was then in full swing, and she and her college sorority sisters formed an auxiliary support unit for our boys over there. They had uniforms, held formation, and marched. It was just the kind of outfit Bettie was looking for.

Leading that unit was the perfect role for Bettie. She was already president of her sorority, and it came as no surprise when the rest of the girls in the auxiliary voted Bettie the leadership position. She loved being "The Colonel" as much as she loved her uniform. Although she remained strong and disciplined, fifty years had passed and she no longer demanded that her friends salute her.

Bettie was different from the other females on campus. Even her eyebrows set her apart. The brows didn't curve, they peaked. They formed a perfect frame for her sometimes green, sometimes black eyes. There was power in those brows. They could send all kinds of messages. Bettie knew that, and so did her kids, as well as all the waiters at her favorite restaurants.

In the twenty-five years I knew her, she was well off financially, and had time to do whatever she wanted to do. Often, when you drove into her driveway, you'd see her down on her knees in some flowerbed or weed patch, depending on her mood. She loved to work in the soil and had to take special care of her hands, which really took a beating. She also had trouble with her knees. Oh, they bent and everything, and didn't give her any pain. But they sagged and she hated that.

She said more than once that if she could find a plastic surgeon who did knee lifts, she'd be in his office the next day. She would also have shelled out a bag of money to any surgeon or diet doctor who could shrink what she called her "big fat stomach." Her wardrobe was built around that stomach. When she went shopping, if she picked out a dress and the stomach said "no", it never got out of the store. She stuck with wide skirts and floppy blouses.

Bettie was addicted to spooks. You know, detective stories, murders, espionage, that genre. If she wasn't feeling well or just wanted to take a day off to stay in bed, she'd trot off to the local library and bring home a shopping bag full of "whodunits" and she'd take them up to her bedroom. There she would sequester herself and read for two days straight, maybe three, coming down only to grab a bite, check her mail, and head back upstairs.

She liked vodka martinis from her pewter shaker. After she'd had a couple, she'd sometimes get a little twinkle in her eyes and if you were with her at the time, you knew that you'd be hurting tomorrow morning, but tonight would be a blast. Those were the nights when the living room rug got rolled up for dancing. If you were there early enough, you might get invited to dinner. It was always the same entrée, at least Bettie always said so: "old, dead chicken."

Some days Bettie would surround herself with crossword puzzles and stay in the kitchen all day testing her vocabulary. When I teased her about spending her day like that, she said, "Wallace Weber...I can do whatever I want. I've earned it!"

Bettie inherited a rich and colorful lexicon from the

small town in eastern Oregon where she grew up.
If everything in her life was going well, she was "happy
as a clam at high tide." If a joke told had any reference
to the male member, it was "his tally whacker." A
relationship that wouldn't last had as much chance as
"a fart on a griddle." And if she thought someone
didn't know what they were talking about, they
"couldn't tell shit from Shinola."

It was at that table in Bettie O'Neal's kitchen when,
over the years, I grew from boyhood to manhood. That
is where I was given insights into the mysterious work-
ings of the female mind. It was there I learned about
such feminine mysteries as the IPL. Had it not been for
those discussions at Bettie's, I would have remained
ignorant of the Invisible Panty Line.

But such knowledge didn't come without a price.
When Bettie got wound up, the vodka martinis kept
coming and the gods of the spirits were toasted often
and with such passion that unless you were an experi-
enced toaster of the gods, you might find yourself STD.
To you uninitiated, that's "Suddenly Taken Drunk."

It happened to me more than once.

Sacred Places

Last week's theme word for my writers' workshop was the word "sacred." I seldom use the word "sacred." It is too broad, too all-encompassing. It's been watered down and misapplied. It stretches from the unknowable and untouchable to the Boy Scout oath.

At one time in my life, I could not go to sacred places. I never liked churches. I didn't go to funerals. The sacred pools of Hawaii were full of litter. If I saw "sacred" on a sign I wanted to misbehave, pee on plaques, wash my hands in holy water, make the Holy Shroud of Jesus into a kite just to watch it fly.

The sacred aspect of Christmas is all but gone. Some argue that as a culture we have outgrown the need for the story of the birth of Christ. What we need now is a new myth to lead us through this millennium. What this myth will look like, no one knows. One thing seems certain: it will have to account for a technology that is expanding at quantum speed while our traditional morality is falling fast behind.

At the risk of sounding cynical, whatever happened to Jesus? Whatever happened to the concept of birth, renewal, hope and a better life? The last time I saw Jesus was in a manger scene on the dashboard of a '63 Chevy. It didn't inspire me to lead a better life or to commit myself to a worthy cause.

You probably have a sacred place or ceremonies of your own that may or may not be related to religion. If so, hang onto them, cherish them. We'll all need them as we make the transition from a mythology of the past to a mythology of the future.

holy moly!

Dear God, how are you? I am fine.
Wish you were here. Please send money.

The Consequences of Adam and Eve

When a Man Marries a Woman

Lucifer's Pyro Park

Easy to Assemble

Encounters with LSD

Situational Deafness

Over the Rainbow

Dear God, how are you? I am fine. Wish you were here. Please send money.

I'm still here in Carmel Valley, muddling my way through. I give myself somewhere between a C+ and a B-.

You know that we've drifted apart since 1955 when I took Philosophy 101 at Washington State. I was teetering on the edge, trying to resurrect what faith I once had. The course examined the major religious philosophies around the globe. When I went home for spring vacation that year my dad expected me to go to church on Sunday. I said "no."

Two years later I took another course which focused on the philosophers themselves, guys like Kant, Kierkegaard, Heidegger, and Descartes. They were tough going for me, but I attended those classes more than others. What I got out of that course was a realization that no matter what philosophy (or mythology) you followed, you may never know God.

Fundamentally it raised the question that I've been trying to answer for years: Who are You, anyway?

When You first met Abraham in the desert, he

asked what You should be called. You said, "I am that I am." What a wonderful expression! We haven't much appreciation for that kind of ego, especially since You warned us to get humble and stay that way. Today the only people who could get away with a line like that are Donald Trump or Popeye!

Keep in touch!

With due respect,

Wally LeValley

The Consequences
of Adam and Eve

We have Adam to thank for consequences.
He started it all. It went like this:

Adam: Whew, another boring day.
Eve: What do you mean, another boring day?
       We just got here. I can still smell the mud.
Adam: One day is just like another. This must be hell.
Eve: It's not hell! It's the Garden of Eden where we
       will commit the first sin.
Adam: What's a sin?
Eve: It's when you go against the wishes of the
       Creator; didn't you listen at the briefing? He
       also told us to go forth and multiply.
Adam: He did? I sort of dozed off a little. I remember
       the multiplying, but I missed the going forth.
       What else did he say?
Eve: He said we'd have dominion over the animals
       and we could eat anything we wanted except
       the fruit from this tree.

Adam: And what will happen if we eat the fruit?

Eve: We'll have to pay the consequences.

Adam: What's a consequence?

Eve: A consequence is what comes after you do something.

Adam: Something—like what?

Eve: Like eating the fruit off the tree.

Adam: So if we never eat off that tree we'll never have consequences?

Eve: Never.

Adam: With no consequences, it's going to be damn boring in this garden. We'll even get bored of multiplying.

Eve: But since we'll never have consequences, we'll never suffer, and we'll never have fights and have to say we're sorry.

Adam: And we'll never have to make moral decisions because there won't be any morality.

Eve: We'll never feel guilt or shame over the choices we make.

Adam: There won't even be any choices, because there won't be any consequences. You can't have one without the other.

Eve: We can just stay here in the garden and practice multiplying.

Adam: And we won't have any consequences?

Eve: Just babies.

Adam: What's a baby?

Eve: It's a little person that looks like us.

Adam: What does it do?

Eve: Well, it fills a lot of diapers.

Adam: What's a diaper, and what fills it with what?

Eve: A diaper is a piece of cloth that you put between the baby's legs so that when it relieves itself it won't soil the garden.

Adam: What do you mean, "soil"?

Eve: You'll see.

Adam: How many babies will there be?

Eve: Billions and trillions and quadrillions. I guess the garden will get pretty crowded.

Adam: An infinite number of babies, an infinite number of diapers? Here? Day after day? Forever?

Eve: All here in the garden.

Adam: Hand me an apple.

When a Man Marries a Woman

When a man marries a woman," the old adage goes, "he hopes she'll never change. When a woman marries a man, she knows he'd better." Which leads me to proffer one generality about the sexes that I cannot support with any scientifically controlled evidence, but I know to be true intuitively: Women thrive on change. Men hate it (unless they initiate it, which is rare).

With women, making changes is built into their genetic code, part of their DNA. This is the same genetic mutation that makes them shop. For them, shopping is a palliative for everything from boredom to post-menopausal depression. The truth is that women don't necessarily shop to buy anything. They go out to shop. To shop means they browse and wander from store to store, taking up the time of the sales people and not making a purchase until the third or fourth visit to the store, if then.

Men simply do not understand that kind of behavior. They feel indecisive if they visit a store more than once for the same item. They secretly think shopping is for morons and masochists, although they never tell their wives that. For men it's simple: women shop, men buy. And so it is.

Let's return to the second part of my thesis: men hate change. They have spent their lives creating an image that will appeal to women. That image is what she fell in love with. You'd think if she were a rational being, she'd take him as is, and do her best to keep him that way. What she's thinking is, "Of course I love him just the way he is. But he could be even better. He's got some rough edges. I'll just help him make a few – 'adjustments'," as she calls them. (Women know that 'change' is a loaded word.) "When I'm finished," she continues, "he'll be twice the man he is now. You won't even recognize him."

Amen to that!

In the meantime, the guy is thinking how much he loves her just the way she is. One day the girl he married with the beautiful long hair comes home with a haircut that would shame a boot Marine. "Jesus Christ! Why did you do that to your hair?" "Because it was time for a change," she says, with her feelings obviously hurt. Tears form and then puddle before splashing down. "I thought you'd welcome the change," she says. Feeling like a jerk, he's speechless. He dare not say more and get in even deeper. He hasn't a clue that this is just a hint of what's to come.

A man must be ever vigilant around the house, especially at dinnertime. There you are at the dinner table, expounding on the situation in Iraq, the involvement of the CIA, the tactics of the insurgents, and the war's effect on international monetary policies. You take a sip of wine, and during the pause she says quietly, "I think I'd like to rearrange the living room." If you let this line go by, you'll be up the proverbial creek in no time. You'll have forfeited your right to go ballistic when you come home from work one day, ready to plop down in your Lazyboy, and you can't find it. It's been assigned a new place in the hall — "to give the room the integrity and balance its energies dictate." That from your wife, who's getting deeper into Feng Shui, which is a plan by a group of powerful Orientals to drive American men over the brink of sanity.

The living room has already been done. Pictures that for years have had their assigned places on the wall, old familiar artifacts like your petrified rock collection, have disappeared. In place of your Lazyboy, you find some bony, Scandinavian thing that dares you to lie down on it.

I like furniture to stay where it belongs. There is enough instability in the world. Everything's moving too fast. We need some things that will stay fixed, permanent, absolute and dependable. Moving a man's furniture nullifies his only chance of achieving order in his own microcosm –that is, his home. Men! It's time to come to your senses and reclaim your territory.

The first thing to do is get rid of that Scandinavian abortion that's supposed to be a couch. Then put the Lazyboy back in its original spot. Finally, go down to your workroom and get your hammer and a handful of six-inch spikes. Now nail your lounger to the floor. Use

the six-inch spikes to go through the base of the
Lazyboy, through the flooring, and into the joists.
That ought to hold it.

True, this will not solve the problem with your wife.
But it will do wonders for your self-esteem.

Lucifer's Pyro Park

Man has always been in awe of fire. From the caves of our ancient ancestors to the present day, no force of nature has been as revered and feared as fire. This was no secret to Dante Alighieri, who, in 1321, published *The Inferno*. It was Dante's imagination, plus a penchant for pyromania, that gave us the unforgettable images of fire and flesh burning endlessly while demons with pitchforks prod sinners in pools of red-hot lava.

Today Dante's vision of hell seems outdated. But it still holds appeal for satirists, fundamental Christians, and interior decorators.

You've probably never read the other two books of *The Divine Comedy*; nobody else has either. *The Paradiso* offers none of the excremental filth, the angst and anguish of the Inferno. In fact, according to *The Paradiso,* once you've had your resume stamped, you can go anywhere and do anything you want, so long as it's boring.

The only real fun you have is the yearly round up of the cherubs. They call it the "Cherub Chase." Heaven is lousy with cherubs. You've seen them in hundreds of pre-Raphaelite and Renaissance paintings. All would-be artists had to take "Cherubs 101" before they moved on to "Perspectives." Furthermore, art schools throughout Italy all used the same models. That's why most of the cherubs look alike on canvas.

Cherubs come in two basic models. First and most popular are the little pink-cheeked, pre-pubescent Pudgies, as they're called. Close behind is the type that looks like middle-aged midgets (some artists hated children). Cherubs would drive even an angel goofy, with their constant fluttering around and prattling about nothing. They give God migraines.

Protestants, by the way, spend little if any time in Purgatory. They are so tight and schedule-oriented, so bound up in the Puritan Ethic, they go straight to hell. They think that once they get there, they'll set things straight, get it organized, and cut Satan in for his percentage. Then, business as usual. As Protestants muster for roll call, the demons are jeering and jumping up and down in the lava pool nearby, laughing their butts off, and chanting, "Time is money, time is money."

A few Christians, who have lived by the Golden Rule throughout their lives, go straight to heaven where they will be feted in style. God knows heaven could use more fetes.

It's hard to describe the tortures Dante came up with to keep his readers on a straight and narrow path to salvation. If you have read *The Inferno*, you always know the deeper you go the worse it gets. Really worse. Sinners are so hideously burned that they wish

to die, but can't. The images are so gruesome, they
would scare the hell out of a Green Beret. Think of
the effect on children.

Rumor has it that Satan is sick of sinners and the
smell of burning flesh. A smell that once tantalized his
taste buds, now gives him acid reflux. He finally knows
what it means to burn.They say he's keeping his staff
with him to open the new enterprise of which he will
be the figurehead, the CEO, and holder of one hundred
percent of the shares. Next year at this time, a big city
on the West Coast will be saturated with signs that
proclaim the good news:

Lucifer's Pyro Park

**Fire and Flames
for the
Whole Family**

(One Sin Will Get You In!)

Easy to Assemble

According to the Book of Genesis in the Old Testament, water is as old as God. At least that's the way I read it. Water was there in the Beginning, on site, when God assumed the role of Creator of an inhabitable planet, something He hadn't tried before. At least, if He had, there's no record of it.

"In the beginning," the story goes, "God created the heaven and the earth." No small task. But before He could go any further, He ran into a problem: What to do with all the water. Water? Read on.

"The earth was without form, and void; and darkness was upon the face of the deep". Here's God, barely underway, and His project is being threatened by an overabundance of H_2O. Frustrated, God issues one of His famous directives: "Let there be light," and there was light, and God liked the effect. For one thing, he could see! For eons He'd been banging His shins in the dark on the scattered harps of sloppy seraphims.

The story continues: He separated the light from

the darkness, and He called the light Day and the dark Night. That was the end of the first day.

The following morning God decided to tackle the water problem full bore. Another directive: "Let there be a firmament in the midst of the waters, and let it divide the waters from the waters." "Waters from waters?" After a day like Day One, at His age God should have rested. He was pooped. He should take a day off. Heck, take two. Take a week. Who's to know?

Where are we? Ah, next God made the firmament, which he could have called the "sky" and saved a lot of confusion. But this is the God of the Old Testament. He had a penchant for archaic vocabulary, and never got a chance to use it.

Finally God hits upon a new idea. He wants to "divide the waters under the firmament from the waters above the firmament." Over the past thousand years, many readers never got past this point in the text.

The next day God plunged into the project with renewed enthusiasm. (Today we'd call Him obsessive compulsive.) So, "God made the firmament and divided the waters which were under the firmament from the waters which were above the firmament. And it was so." There's nothing left to say when something ends, "And it was so." It's so final.

You have to admire God's spunk. Who'd stick with a plan that says stuff like "separate the waters from the waters?" Maybe a nuclear physicist. It would drive any hydrologist to drink.

It was the end of Day Two, and as far as we need to go. God had His waters separated, but the system still had problems. For one thing, water was not always a benefit to man. (See Noah, where God damn near drowned His creation.) Or, see the river flow into your house. (See the awkward transition to the next paragraph.)

Like water, the Bible has been trickling through the Far East since introduced by well-meaning Portuguese missionaries about four hundred years ago. It now appears in translation alongside Machiavelli's *Prince* in the desk drawers of some of the most powerful manufacturers in Japan and China. They have grown wealthy by following God's example in the part of Genesis above. You've seen their credo on products exported to the West thousands of times, especially if you're a do-it-yourselfer. It reads: "Easy to assemble, Follow simple instructions."

God has a perverse sense of humor.

Encounters — A Night with LSD

The first time I took LSD was with a dancer named Jan who worked at Bimbo's Night Club in San Francisco. Jan had taken LSD before and was going to guide me through the night in case I saw anything I couldn't handle.

We dropped the acid about 6:00 p.m. at her place, and we waited. After ten minutes, I got impatient. Nothing was happening. "Maybe you got burned," I said.

"Don't worry, it's good," she said.

So we lay there on the floor sipping cheap wine, waiting.

I was about to call the night a bust and go home, when the knotholes in the pine ceiling began to drift around. It was as if the ceiling was made of a series of overlays, like they used in math classes. It was scary. My reality didn't seem as steady as I thought it was. A little later the walls started to breathe when I breathed. I felt great. Life was beautiful. Life was the grand adventure. There was nothing to fear. So why had I let fear drive my life, I thought. I'd like to send some of this stuff to Mom. In fact, I wanted everyone to share this experience. The whole country, the entire nation, turned on.

By now the walls were pulsing in sync with my heartbeat, which was amazingly calm. I was still lying on the floor, intrigued by the floating designs on the ceiling, when, out of nowhere, a kitten emerged and announced itself with a couple of mews. Then, swear to God, it came over to me and lay down across my neck, right on my throat, two paws on one side, two on the other. It snuggled up and began to purr. Usually I would have pulled him off and shooed him away. But I was somehow caught by the vibration I felt coming from the kitten. I could feel the purring, not just hear it. I felt it purring in me.

Time passed, and this question popped into my head: "What is there in a kitten's purr that echoes the mystic motor of the universe?" I said the line out loud for Jan. She lit another stick of incense and smiled. I thought I was onto something. Then I realized it wasn't a question to be answered. A piece of graffiti on a phone booth wall in North Beach said it all: "Life is not a problem to be solved. It is a mystery to be lived."

After a while the kitten got up and left. By then I was hiking up the side of a cone-shaped mountain, like Mt. Fuji without the snow. I had an appointment with God at the top.

When I got to the top, God wasn't there. He'd been there, but He'd moved on into the clouds hanging over the mountain. Once again I had missed Him. Then Jan came floating by, her feet not touching the ground. She was still wearing that reassuring smile when she stopped a little above me, suspended in the air. I got a feeling that she could have risen higher if I wasn't with her. To me, she was a bodhisattva, an enlightened being who could go straight to God but chose to stay back and help others cross over.

I wondered, how can she float? I couldn't float. And she rose higher than I did. She went clear off the mountain. Suddenly I knew. She believed in the higher good, absolute reality, Allah, call it what you will. She believed, while I thought. That made all the difference.

Next day, off the acid, I was still wondering what the whole scene on the mountain was trying to teach me. I decided that my analytical mind had held me back. The intellect alone could bring you just so far, no matter how smart you are. You had to make the leap of faith. I couldn't make it. Jan did.

The intellect alone will never get me to God. No matter how many books I read, whose philosophy or whose discipline I follow, I'll never get there. I could shave my head and go to an ashram and meditate for the rest of my life, and still not experience whatever God is. Yet a part of me will not give up. I need to expand my definition of God. That much is clear. That feeling was disappointing but not devastating. It was as close as I'd ever be to feeling at home in the universe.

I learned these three things during that acid trip:

1) The universe is the mind of God;
2) There is nothing to fear;
3) There is nowhere else to go.

Let me illustrate that number 3. During the night

with Jan and LSD, I had another image I forgot to tell you about. Someone was cutting my hair, straight across the back like Prince Val or the little Dutch boy. Once a piece of hair was cut, it wouldn't fall. There was no up or down. There was no frame of reference. Just a chair sitting in space. The hair couldn't fall, nor could it rise. It was all one, the hair, the scissors, the barber, and me.

When we started coming down about 5:00 a.m., we were both tired and a bit jittery, like we'd been up all night on coffee, writing a term paper. Other than that we were feeling good. I felt like I could never really die. No one could. I thought about my high school chemistry class, where I learned we are 98% water. Whether you get put in the earth to slowly decay, or incinerated into vapor and ash, 98% of your body will, sooner or later, be available to the Life Source. After all, we are mainly hydrogen, oxygen, nitrogen, and carbon, plus a few minerals like potassium and manganese, all of which will be freed to recombine at random anywhere in the universe. I take solace from that.

I don't want to be reincarnated. I don't want to be resurrected. I just hope that, when the time comes, I'll be ready to be recycled.

Situational Deafness

My wife suffers from "Situational Deafness" "SD"). If you haven't heard of it yet, it's a condition that has been misdiagnosed for years and is just now getting the notice of medical journals, including that of the AMA.

It seems that audiologists have discovered a previously unknown gland near the base of the cerebellum in quadrant three which is the location of the nerves controlling the sense of hearing. Through some mysterious mental process, an adult female can turn this gland into a sort of on/off switch. The switch, if you will, is a kind of rheostat she can adjust from low to high as she pleases. Let me give you an example of how it works.

I'm not one of those people who talk during a movie in a theater. But in my living room, I may make a few comments on what we're watching, especially when I feel like sharing my insights on the program we're seeing. I may say something like, "This is a lot of crap," or, "How can anyone watch this drivel?" I guess that last one is what's called a rhetorical question: it never gets an answer.

I like to critique the programs we watch together. It's my job. I puzzle out the most intricate plots out loud. It's fun to share.

If I've been in another room, I politely ask for a quick synopsis of the plot. "Where are we? What's happened? Who's that guy?" Things like that. Earlier in our marriage twenty-some years ago when her hearing was still good, I would have gotten a response to those questions, but since this deafness came on, all I get are limited sounds like "huh?" and "shhhh!"

The sad thing is that not only does she have S.D., but she is also strung out on TV, which exacerbates her condition. Her current passion is "American Idol". Why that, who knows? Addicts don't need a reason.

I do my best to drum up some enthusiasm for the program. But it's hard to stay enthusiastic when your wife has turned deaf and she's lying on the couch in the fetal position as she watches her program. I get nervous and feel abandoned, and start talking even more. I ask questions about character, mood, atmosphere, setting, and theme. Doesn't everybody? Questions like these during the program help us feel connected, help us benefit from what in the 90's was known as "quality time."

Let me offer another example of her addictive behavior. Two weeks ago we were having a great vacation in Arizona. After a full day of sightseeing in the red rock country around Sedona, we decided to check into our motel and rest before going out to dinner. As soon as we had checked in, she asked the desk clerk what time "American Idol" came on. The clerk said he didn't know. He said he didn't watch it. My wife gave him that quizzical look that says, "Are you an idiot, or what?" Then she turned to me and said, "Let's find someone else, they'll know."

She asked the kid outside parking cars. He said he'd never heard of "American Idol." He asked, "What is it?" She answered, "Never mind," and walked off. At the restaurant she queried the hostess, the waitress, and the busboy. None of them had the foggiest notion of what time the program started, or even if it was shown in that part of Arizona.

By now that look of panic had settled in her eyes. It was easy to recognize. I'd seen it plenty of times before. It always made me nervous, sometimes fearful. When we lived in Mexico and she'd get that look in her eye, our Mexican neighbors would call their children in. They liked her well enough, but they were intimidated by what they called "El Ojo De Muerte" ("The Eye of Death"). It was the look that came into an addict's eyes just before she either went ballistic or shrunk back into the abyss.

So we went to the room and she began to desperately surf the channels. She was losing hope and getting ready for bed at 7:00, even though there would be light for two more hours. She got into bed and pulled the cover over her head. I retired to the bathroom so I could read without a light bothering her.

A few minutes later I heard her make some sort of guttural sound and throw the covers off the bed. When

I went back into the room she was trying the channels for one last time.

And lo and behold, there was Ryan Seacrest, the MC for "American Idol" leering out from the center of the screen.

Thank God! A fix! She stopped hyperventilating and some color came back into her cheeks. She was getting what she needed to make it through the night.

I said, "Is that good luck, or what?" No answer. She had gone deaf. She was kneeling before the TV like a Zen student before an electric Buddha. Her day had been a success after all.

As for me, I spent the night in the bathroom reading "Ulysses".

Over the Rainbow

.I've never had a flying dream, at least none that
I recall. Freud would say I'm so anal retentive I couldn't
stand the freedom of flight. Those of a religious bent
would tell me I lack faith that the air would support
me. They've got a point. I can still see the disciples
trying to walk on water.

Leonardo was nuts about flight. He studied its
principles and knew more about it than anyone on the
planet. He built a set of wings for man to fly with, but
they didn't work. He sacrificed more than one appren-
tice in his attempts to get airborne. But it was not
much later that someone figured out that a man
would need a sternum of grotesque proportions in
order to fly by beating his own wings.

Years ago I spent a day watching seabirds.
I marveled at the pelicans riding the thermals a few
inches above the water so effortlessly. Even the
seagulls looked graceful hovering above the fishing
boats in the harbor. "How easy to ride and hover,

when you're a bird," I thought. But before I yielded to reverie, my cynical side crept in. It said, "Those birds don't know they're flying. They just do it. They're neither happy nor sad with their lot. It's us who feel a longing because we're unable to fly, and we know it." Hearing that took the edge off my envy, but it didn't leave me satisfied.

If you want some idea of how it feels to be a bird, try gliding. Gliders ride the thermals off the hills like pelicans off the sea. The only sound is the air rushing by the cabin. You can soar and swoop like the gulls. It's as if you're being supported by some magic force.

I remember my last glider flight. When we were high enough to level off, we spotted what was left of a rainbow in a valley a few miles west. It was a rare experience. When it's warm enough to glide, it's usually too warm for rainbows. But there it was, for a few moments more.

I thought about that fading rainbow later and Noah came to mind after the Great Flood when the waters were receding. God came to Noah as a rainbow, assuring Noah that He, God, was still with him, connected to him as a rainbow connects two points on the horizon, or, more pointedly, the rainbow connects heaven and earth.

The spirit of that meaning of rainbows is lost to us now. Centuries ago we turned God into a pot of gold. Less spiritual, but more practical.

When Judy Garland, late in her life, sang "Over the Rainbow" at Carnegie Hall, something wonderful transpired. She brought an entire audience of sophisticated adults with her as she went in search of the land that she heard of "once in a lullaby." "Somewhere out there," she says, "dreams really do come true." That's the eternal promise of the rainbow, the hope it offers. Yet at the end of the song the tone shifts and presents that eternal question: "If such a land exists, and others go there, why, oh why, can't I?"

dry ink...

Finding My Voice

Writing and Why I Didn't

From a Writer's Diary

Wee Tim'rous Beastie

Finding My Voice

The last time I enjoyed writing I was a broke and lonely Marine. That was on Oahu over forty years ago. I had no money, no car, no prospects. Even Sears wouldn't give me credit to buy a bike. Life was the pits.

Finding myself with no money and nothing to do, I read a book. No big deal for most of you, but a very big deal for me. I never read. I avoided books. I mean, I could read, but I didn't. Then one day, a fellow Marine gave me a crumpled copy of *On The Road*. That book opened the world for me.

I wanted to share my discovery with a friend on the mainland and another in the Navy in Japan. We called it the "Triangle" and wrote long rambling letters, full of youth and enthusiasm, and sent them off across the Pacific. I was excited by my writing and the books we were sharing.

After I got out of the Marines, I went back to college and became an English teacher, one of life's little ironies. It would be twenty years before I wrote again. Then I took a course called "Writing for Publication" from the local college. Luckily (or maybe not) I sold the first four class assignments to the local newspaper. I thought, this is easy. I could make a living doing this. So I took a year's leave from the high school where I'd been teaching, and became a "writer."

There is a little building on my property that sits beside the river. I set it up as my "studio." It was perfect. No noise, no phones, no distractions of any kind. Nothing to be done but write.

Within a month, I hated it.

What I had sold to the local paper were nonfiction articles. "How To" articles, "Where To Go" articles, and a brief biography of an artist. Informative? Yes. Truthful? Of course. Exciting? Not a bit.

I was trying to crack into the magazine market, and getting nowhere. The frustration of trying to guess what would sell, then struggling to give them the kind of articles they said they wanted, could drive you to drink.

In six months I sold one article to a camping magazine about the disappearance of the American front porch. I got a check for $150.00. I estimated my income to be a little over four cents an hour, not counting the coffee breaks.

One day a friend of mine named Alex called me after reading a story I wrote about a men's group. It was the early 80's and the men's movement was in full swing. He called to give me his unsolicited critique of the article. That was Alex. "Walls," he said, "why don't you write like you talk? I can't hear you in this article." I resented the comment. Didn't he realize I was trying to be objective, stay out of the story, and just present the material as clearly as I could? Besides, what the hell did he know about writing?

In the back of my mind I knew he was right. I wasn't writing anything I cared about. I just wanted to write what would sell, and justify my taking a year off. There was absolutely no "me" in there, in any of my articles. What was missing was what writers call a "voice."

I was getting dangerously depressed. I couldn't take the lack of response from the editors. I couldn't take the loneliness, or the rejection either. Some writers could, I couldn't. Eventually I gave up.

Now, twenty-four years after my writing experiment in the hut by the river, I don't have to sell. I don't have to sweat a grade. I don't have to write what some editor might want to hear. For the first time since Hawaii over forty years ago, I'm having fun writing. And I'm finally finding my voice.

Writing and Why I Didn't

I don't write novels. I never did. For an English teacher that's a little hard to admit. But English teachers don't write novels, at least not the ones I know.

I went off to college to study journalism. Like Hemingway, I had success writing for the high school newspaper. And since that was the only way I could see my name in print, I thought I'd give journalism a try.

I lasted on the college paper less than a year. I simply didn't have a need to write. There was no burning desire. Journalism was just another course.

Six years later, after three years in the Marines, I returned to college as a creative writing major. In the Marines, I had found a love of books and writers. I was electrified by Jack Kerouac. On The Road affected me at the level of my soul. "Yes, yes, dig America. Go. See. Do. Live."

And then I discovered Hemingway and fell completely under his existential code and macho mentality. And his style, whether it came from Gertrude Stein or

Sinclair Lewis, as some critics argued, I didn't care. I just know that passages of his books would pop into my head at odd times as he was sinking into my psyche.

As for myself, I was writing letters filled with desperate energy to people back home. Reading a stack of those letters saved by a friend over the years and recently sent to me, I was saddened by their content. Was I ever that optimistic, that sure of myself?

What happened to the young man who was so confident that there was a meaning to life, that if you looked hard enough, it made sense? Where did I lose the confidence that I had something to say?

I guess when I changed my major from creative writing to English, I took the road most traveled. And, as the poet said, that made all the difference.

From a Writer's Diary

"Write something, God dammit! That's what you're here for." All my well-tuned undergraduate excuses for not doing a writing assignment are alive and well (notice the word "assignment"—that word alone can take the joy out of writing.)

I'm forcing this piece of prose through by sheer discipline. You know, you decided to stay home and study rather than go out drinking with your buddies. That's called "deferred pleasure" in Psych 101. It's a mark of maturity, they say. I have had little experience with that myself.

It's not the subject of children that bothers me. After all, we've written on air, rainbows, celebrations, and hats. No, it's not the subject that's bugging me. It's me.

I feel like I'm in my undergraduate days when a term paper was coming due and I hadn't given it a thought. The closer the deadline drew, the more I resented it. I proudly bore the slings and arrows of devout procrastination.

I still approach most assignments the same way I did in college. First I balance my typewriter. This may or may not involve adjusting the floor joists, but it will require some time. It's a very old typewriter and crotchety as hell. Then I arrange my desk (no writer can produce clarity out of chaos). Several things have to be done before I write, one of which is to separate the small from middle-sized paperclips. This is a must. If I'm lucky, it can take me the whole morning.

After I finish my pre-writing warm-up I have to start writing. But—it's too late in the day now, so I'll hold off until tomorrow so I can get off to a good start.

In the morning I grab a cup of coffee and go to "the hut." I insert a clean sheet of paper into the typewriter, take a deep breath, and sit up straight. I'm now ready for a visit from the muses, or simply the challenge of the day. I wait for inspiration.

Then I see the spider web. What a beauty. During the night, some arachnid has structured his personal paradigm from the wall to the back of the typewriter. My God, what patience, what symmetry, what symbolism! Yes, symbolism. There's something eerie here. Is this a message for me? Are there, as I have suspected for years, forces that do not want me to use this machine or anything like it? Will my touch violate its sanctity? Is the web an omen telling me my writing will never really fly? My prose postmortem? And why a web, why a spider? Why not a butterfly or a hummingbird? Who's trying to get my attention? What are they trying to say?

I look at the clock. It's time to call it a day. "Always leave a little in the well," Hemingway said. "Don't empty it in a day, hold something back for morning." I know what he meant. For a writer, there's no hell like a dry well!

"Wee Tim'rous Beastie"

It's a well-known fact that poets come off the line
with a part missing — or maybe a part extra. Who
knows? They look just like normal people, so they're
hard to spot, unless of course they are speaking in
rhymes, which they're likely to do. They also see
metaphors everywhere. They can't help it. They're
born that way.

Poets do strange things. One, a guy named
McLeish, was walking home from the college where he
taught poetry, when he spotted a fresh gopher mound
on his neighbor's lawn. Most of us would go get a
trap. But this McLeish goes over and sits down by the
gopher hole. He just sits there, like he's listening for
something. Then he starts talking into the gopher hole.
This is in broad daylight where several people could see
him. But not one person tried to stop him. Poets can
be dangerous, especially when talking to gophers.

As I said, poets aren't like us. To prove my case,
I'll tell you another story, although you probably won't

believe it. But he published the poem. It's in lots of books, so you know it's true. This Scotsman named Burns is out plowing his field, and his plow takes the roof right off a den full of mice. Does he stomp the little grain eaters into the ground and keep on plowing, like he should? Remember, he's a poet—so he stands there for a while over Mrs. Mouse and her offspring. He says he was thinking about the similarities between the critter's situation and his own. And then he goes home and writes a poem about it. By the time he's through poeting, he's decided the mouse is better off than himself! I told you you wouldn't believe it. The poem, entitled "To a Mouse", starts like this:

> *Wee, sleekit, cowrin', tim'rous beastie,*
> *O, what a panic's in thy breastie!*

He's speaking to a mouse, for God's sake! A Scottish mouse. A few lines later he calls the mouse:

> *...earthborn companion*
> *An' fellow mortal!*

See what he's doing here? He's poeting. "Fellow mortal", poppycock! A man is a man, and a mouse is a mouse, and the latter will never be kin to me. He goes on. He reminds the mouse that man (or mouse) proposes, but God disposes, or, as the poet puts it,

> *The best laid schemes o'mice an' men*
> *Gang aft agley.*

I have to admit he was onto something there. There's truth in that. Then he muddies it all up in the last stanza:

> *Still thou art blest, compared wi' me,*
> *The present only toucheth thee;*
> *But och! I backward cast my e'e*
> > *On Prospects drear!*
> *An' forward, though I canna see,*
> > *I guess an' fear!*

I here, you see that poet took a simple thing like plowing into a mouse house and built it into something bigger, and he ends up being ashamed of himself. Who but a poet would compare himself to a mouse, and come out on the losing end?

one year at a time...

Waiting to be Called

According to Freud, the one thing a man must have to give his life meaning is his work. That phrase has intimidated me for years. "His work" looks so simple here on the page. It's far from it. "His work" went beyond jobs and employment. It meant a focus, passion for what you were pursuing, what drove you, what centered your life.

Somewhere years back I read that less than one percent of all who work love what they do. That was no surprise to me. Over the years I have become increasingly aware of how few people I've met who can say they love what they do for a living.

I'm not willing to go as far as Thoreau in his assertion that "most men live lives of quiet desperation." But my experience in factories and the service would support his assertion: work without passion is drudgery. Alex Weygers of Carmel Valley was a Renaissance man, a twentieth century Leonardo. In his 80's, he said, "I can hardly wait for the sun to come up so I can start my day, to see what lies before me." For Alex, the word "job" was not in his vocabulary. "Job" implied fitting into some structure bigger than yourself, finding your slot, your niche. Like it or not, you were always replaceable.

But the person who loves what he does for a living cannot be replaced. There is no one else quite like him, and there is something in him, perhaps a passion, perhaps his genius as Emerson called it, something that cannot be absorbed by anything larger than itself, not the company or the corporation or the culture or the society.

The closest I ever got to that kind of work was years ago as a counselor in a camp for teenagers. It was in the Santa Cruz Mountains above Soquel. I was fresh out of the Marine Corps and looking for what to do with the rest of my life. I hadn't given much thought to the future, especially going back to college. I didn't know what to study. I certainly had no passion to teach. And yet being a camp counselor for teenage boys brought out a flair for teaching I never knew I had.

There we were, nine of us in an old, open-sided Army tent for the summer. It was the only job I ever had where I got to use my entire personality. Whatever skills I had were all needed and appreciated by the staff and the campers. I doubt Freud would have considered one summer's experience as "my work" in the sense that it was some deep and lasting thing. All I know is that was forty years ago and I still remember it clearly— and often with longing.

Partly because of that summer's experience, I later decided to become a teacher. In the Marines I had discovered books and the joy of reading. I decided if I could combine my newfound gift for working with teenagers and my love of books, I could be teaching English. To keep myself in school, I ran nightclub tours of North Beach in San Francisco. There was no GI Bill in those days. I was on my own, living the life of a medieval scholar, readying myself to start my teaching career.

When I got my credential, I found a job at Carmel High School. Two major differences between being a camp counselor and being a teacher soon made themselves apparent. (1) Most of the kids I had at camp grew to love it and didn't want it to end. Conversely, too many of the kids I had in class didn't want to be there. (2) Just because I loved books didn't mean my students would. Many of them never read anything at all. Here I was in Carmel, California, the "cultural center" of the Central Coast, and not one student in my freshman class had read *Cannery Row*. In fact, they hadn't read any Steinbeck at all.

For reasons I won't go into now, I stayed at that job (not my work, my job) for seventeen years. It wasn't my bliss, but I didn't know what else to do.

I kept waiting to be called to do something, real man's work, God's work; it didn't matter as long as I could throw myself into it.

I'm still waiting.

Dear Evynn
(A letter to my daughter when she went off to college)

When I first went off to college, I really didn't know what I was there for. Auburn, Washington, the small town where I spent my last two years of high school, didn't offer much to graduates. As I remember it, you could stay around town at some flunky, go-nowhere job, work in canneries (when they worked), go in the service, or, if your folks had any money, go to college.

Since the first three options weren't appealing to me, and since my dad offered to pay half the costs, I went off to Washington State. Three of my friends and I went through rush, and we all pledged the same fraternity. Joining a fraternity was my first mistake, although I didn't know it at the time. It was "the thing to do," and so I did it.

You had to get at least a two point in your first semester to be formally initiated into the frat. I got a 2.8, which was enough.

A year and a half later I'd had it with fraternity life. I moved into an old house across town. There were five of us, one of whom was a veteran from the Korean War. He believed in college and went to class regularly, unlike the rest of us. We all got along well, but by the end of that year at WSC, I swore to God I was through with college. Forever. I felt like Holden Caulfield. I didn't know what I was doing in school, so I packed my stuff and went home to Auburn.

By the end of the summer I was desperate for friends. All of my old buddies were in the canneries, the service, or off at college. They weren't around town. With my dad's help, I was able to register late at the University of Washington in Seattle. This change in geography, I told myself, would rekindle my desire for higher education. That lasted for a few short weeks. Then I started skipping classes and assignments. By Christmas of that year, I was drinking too much and driving suicidally. I was fat and miserable. Once again, nothing made sense. I needed a dramatic change, and fast. So I joined the Marines.

After three years in the corps, I felt much better about myself. I had gained some self-discipline and self-respect in the Marines. I owe them that.

After discharge in San Francisco, I hooked up with Gary Kellard, and old friend from Washington State. He rounded up three of his old frat brothers, and the five of us got an apartment. Guys moved in and out, but Gary and I kept that apartment together for two years. I was always proud of that.

One night Gary and I were sitting in my room pondering such questions as "What are you going to do with the rest of your life?" Gary was currently hooked into a go-nowhere job as a film booker for San Francisco theaters.

Before the night was over, we both decided to become English teachers. This was a real surprise for me. In high school and in the first three years of college I hated to read. My folks never read anything either. There were no books around our house. If my class could have voted, I would have been the least likely to become a teacher of any kind. Fortunately I'd had some experiences since dropping out of college that made the goal seem possible.

One thing happened in the Marines. That's where I started to read. I read the writers I'd never read in school. I was twenty-two years old and just beginning to get literate. A simple case of arrested development.

The second influence on my decision to teach was a summer I spent being a camp counselor. That was the best job I ever had. It used all of my talents. I did things I didn't know I could do. I was appreciated for who I was. What a blessing to finally feel good about yourself, and find that you've got some things to offer!

The night Gary and I were trying to decide what to do with ourselves, my future began to take shape, and it was exciting. I put my enjoyment of working with teenagers as a camp counselor together with my newfound love of books, and I thought, why not do both? Work with teenagers and talk about books. So that's how it happened.

I guess I wrote this letter to show you how it was

with me. Whatever you do, I know you'll do well.

I want you to know this house is always open to you. So is my heart.

Love,

Dad

Just Another Student

It had no business being there scrawled in the margin of the essay. It was a silly line: "I AM NOT A BAD KID!" But for a long time after I first saw it, I had trouble getting it out of my mind.

It was on the rough draft of a student's paper. Normally I don't read rough drafts. I just ask that they be attached to the final copy of the assignment so that I have some evidence of the preparatory work. I'm not sure what made me look at this one, but I wished I hadn't.

Before the line caught my eye, the girl who wrote it had been just another hostile student. She was sixteen, bright, pretty, and sarcastic. She was also a pain. There was a kind of cynicism about her that made most of what I was doing in class seem superfluous. I didn't like her much.

We both knew our roles, and as long as we played them well, we'd get through the semester without incident. But now, with one scrawled sentence, she had stepped out of character.

I can still see the line. It had been written in capital letters and finished with an exclamation point. It was as if, during the writing of the rough draft, the recollection of some previous hurt had suddenly crowded its way up from her subconscious and forced her to defend herself.

The line was incongruous. Next to her neat penmanship and fluid prose, it was out of place. It sounded like a protest from a pouting seven-year-old, not a precocious sixteen-year-old. And she was precocious in many ways.

Physically she had reached maturity early. She was sexy, stylish, and socially at ease. She was looked up to by other girls in the class, and the boys treated her with silent awe. She was too far beyond them, and they knew it. As a student, her insights into literature were impressive, and so was her ability to express herself. She could have easily carried her weight in a much more difficult course. Her questions often forced me to examine aspects of a work that I had passed by too quickly, or had never considered before. In that one regard I liked having her in class.

But her cynicism too often set the tone for other students, especially for the girls who emulated her style and sophistication. She was too much of a negative force. Had she been a more positive kind of student, she could have been a great help to me. But positive she wasn't, and I often wished that she had been enrolled in someone else's section, not mine.

Unfortunately, the negativity and cynicism never slackened; in fact, they even seemed to increase, at times approaching blatant disrespect of me as teacher. But she somehow always knew when she had gone as far as limits would allow. I made a habit of checking her rough drafts on later essays. I never again found anything of a personal nature scrawled in the margins. Eventually, I dismissed her "I AM NOT A BAD KID!" as a moment of frustration. Finally, I put it out of my mind entirely.

We continued our adversarial relationship throughout the rest of the semester. Then we broke for summer vacation. I never saw her again after that and haven't really thought about her until this day. I'm not even sure what brings her to mind.

It doesn't really matter. In the long run she was just another student. I don't remember her name.

A Bone Through the Nose

I tried to define beauty once. I was in over my head from the beginning. I was team-teaching a high school humanities course with a friend of mine. We were examining Greek culture, specifically a statue by Phidias that was on the projection screen. It had been there only a few seconds, when some kid in the back asked rather snidely, "So what's so beautiful about that?" That question, as well as his tone of voice, started the whole thing.

We had some students who loved art and we began by trying to determine what made that statue beautiful. We ended up arguing for the rest of the period. The next day we started over, and we came up with three criteria for beauty: symmetry, balance, and harmony. At least they would do for a start. Having settled that for the moment, we were about to move on when the same kid piped up with, "Shouldn't we define our terms before we try to apply them?"

It took two full hours to get any sort of agreement

on those three seemingly simple words. This definition was taking more time than we thought it should, but we started it and didn't see how to get out gracefully.

Over thirty years ago a failed stockbroker from L.A. named Jack moved to Carmel Valley and changed his name to Juan. Juan made his living in the Valley by doing odd jobs and repairs. He was good and he was honest and many people sought him out at first. On his business card it said, "Projects begun with enthusiasm." He didn't always finish the job, but he began it with the best of intentions.

Unlike Juan, my colleague and I couldn't just walk off. We envied Juan's style. We were beginning to lose enthusiasm for our project. After arriving at some understanding of our three terms, we ran into another question: Is beauty absolute, or is it culturally defined? In other words, how can something be beautiful in one culture but not in another?

At our first attempt to answer these questions, we placed on the screen a photo from National Geographic of a young African woman who had a three-inch saucer embedded in her lower lip. In her tribe, it was the custom of all women of marriageable age. It was considered the height of feminine beauty. To us, it was grotesque.

Another picture showed a young man with a four-inch bone sticking through his nose. Its function was to attract a bride. All white and shiny, it too was considered beautiful.

We finally had to agree that not all aspects of beauty could pass the cross-cultural test. Even so, we still believed in our definition. We arranged for a well-known local psychologist to join us the following day. He was a devotee of Carl Jung who was best known for his theory of the collective unconscious. The collective unconscious, Jung argued, was like an ancient depository of early man's dreams and myths and legends. These early stories he called archetypes, were shared throughout man's history, and appeared all over the world, in places diverse and isolated.

For instance, the story of the flood in the Old Testament existed in slightly modified forms throughout the world long before it found its way into the book of Genesis. The hero of the virgin birth whose father is a god goes back thousands of years before Christ. We have a common gene pool, in essence, a common ancestry of these archetypical stories. If dreams, myths, and legends were part of the collective unconscious, then surely certain aspects of beauty were also cross-cultural and common to us all.

We knew that our methods were suspect and open to question. But we didn't have the time, or the expertise, to pursue the project any further.

It took James Joyce a hundred plus pages to lay out his theory of aesthetics in *Portrait of the Artist as a Young Man*. We spent three days, and gave it up. I'm sure Juan would understand.

Two Days in the Classroom

As a substitute at the local high school, every once in a while I put some quotation on the board just to see how the kids will react. Sometimes they don't react at all. Sometimes I get lucky.

One day I wrote "It is better to do evil than do nothing," a line borrowed from Montaigne. It brought up some discussion of morality, ethics and religion. Not a bad hour for a sub, but I wanted more. It was a two-day assignment, so towards the end of a dull hour the next day I wrote, "Our technology has outstripped our morality." Another borrowed line, I forget the source. But I remember the class reaction.

"What does it mean?" asked a boy, usually too shy to speak in class.

"It means," I started out, "that technologically we're moving too fast for our own good."

"Outstripped whose morality? Not mine!"
This from a girl in the back of the room who liked to sabotage subs. It got a few laughs, but I plugged on.

"What the quote says," I said, "is that we spend too much time and money going outward, and too little going in."

The class was looking a bit puzzled.

"I'll give you an example," I continued. "Putting a man on the moon in the sixties cost the country two hundred billion dollars in the final year of the space program. The same year, Congress cut spending on mental health by thirty percent. Get the implication, anybody?"

"Sort of," offered one unusually quiet girl. "It's easier to go out there and challenge the frontiers than it is to go inside ourselves?" I liked this girl.

"Nicely put," I said. "And what do we mean by 'out there'?" I asked.

"Out there," she said. "You know, we're Americans. We pride ourselves in being king of the technological mountain. We invent the stuff the world consumes." She was an articulate student. I was thankful. "In Econ," she said, "we talk about gross national product, balance of trade, and the national debt. Truth is, we produce so we can feel good about ourselves. What makes me mad is that we could solve mental health problems, like schizophrenia, epilepsy, and Alzheimer's, if we'd only stop trying to prove that we're the biggest, best, most powerful nation on earth."

"But," said a big kid in a letterman's jacket, "consuming is what it's all about. Consuming is fun. It's why I work."

"Yes," I replied, "it is fun and it makes us feel

good. But it's too easy."

"What do you mean 'too easy'?" he asked. "We have to pay for cell phones, palm pilots, CD players, pagers, computers, and all the stuff that goes with 'em. Something new comes out every day, it's hard to keep up!"

"I know, it's a burden," I responded with just a bit of sarcasm slipping out, "but the computer you buy today will be obsolete next year, if not next month. Where does it end? How do we slow down? What's the hurry?"

"Look at the cell phone," I continued. "It's ubiqui- tous. That's a big word for 'everywhere at all times'. From where you sit you can call someone in another room, even though the school has a zero tolerance for cell phones and I'll have to confiscate yours if you use it in class," I said, this time with a smile. I was trying to inject a little humor.

There was a slight rustling sound as several students tried to sneak their phones into their backpacks.

"There is never a moment," I said, "when we have to be alone. Some device, like the cell phone or the pager or the portable CD player, is always there to ward off the silence. We use our electronic toys to make us feel better, to fill the void inside us. We can't stand silence. It scares us."

That was enough for the class wiseass. "Aren't you swinging pretty far outside your area of expertise? This is an English class, not philosophy or economics." His tone always pissed me off.

I ignored him. I was on a roll and didn't want to stop. I gave it one more shot. "The quote means,"

I said, returning to my theme, "that man will always accept physical danger, challenge the boundaries, knock down the walls, because it's easier and safer than going into himself and seeking the essence of what he is. When Richard Nixon was President of the United States and we landed on the moon, he said on national television, 'This is every American's greatest hour.' Not mine. I couldn't buy it. I couldn't ever get behind the hero stuff. To me, those astronauts were dedicated, highly trained technicians who had success-fully completed their mission. That was it."

I wasn't finished yet. "If you want to be heroic, take a tour of the dark and scary places inside your head. Consider: why are we still blowing the legs off little children? Why do we keep making and selling land mines? Why is man the only animal that hates? What's hidden in our heart of darkness? Who are we?"

The class had grown silent.

"The most heroic thing you can do right now is to shut up. Be silent. Stop babbling. Listen for your inner voice. Who are you, really? What is serious? That's the question. You won't find the answer at the mall. You'll find it only in yourself."

I was breaking into a light sweat and my heart had picked up a beat or two. It was one of those rare moments in teaching when you feel like you're doing something important, something of value. Standing in front of the class, I began to realize that in my enthusi-asm, or rapture, I had taken over and brought an end to discussion. The Socratic method of teaching by questioning had been tossed out the window. But at the moment I didn't care. I was a teacher, and for the first time in years, I felt like one.

Finally the bell rang and the students filed out. I had no class the next period. The room was quiet. I sat there in the silence feeling good about myself. Maybe for one kid, in this one class, in this one small town in America, I had, as the saying goes, "made a difference." As a teacher, you seldom knew.

swing shift...

Pantywaist Howard

Life After Youth

Indoctrination: Once was Enough

Mr. Macho

The Autumn of My Life

Pantywaist Howard

When I was in the fourth grade, my girl friend
Toni and I were at what might be called a "crossroads
in the relationship." We had been going steady for
several weeks. She had been wearing my all-metal
Captain Midnight decoder ring on a chain around her
neck, even though the ring turned the neck of her
sweaters black.

Everything was going well until, one day, along
came Howard, the new kid. Howard was a pantywaist.
I could make Howard yell Uncle every time we wrestled
at recess. But even though Howard was a pantywaist,
Toni liked him. One day at recess, I overheard her say,
"Gee, Howard, you're really sweet." I don't know what
they'd been doing, but what Toni said gave me a jolt of
what I later learned to be jealousy.

Toni and Howard got even friendlier, until I couldn't
stand it anymore. It was time for Toni to make a choice,
no doubt the most important choice she would ever
have to make. So I wrote her a letter laying out my

grievance. I told her that either she wanted to be my girlfriend, or not. Me...or Howard. Choose.

It was a good letter, impressive in its bold number two pencil on wide-spaced newsprint. There was no doubt in my mind that this letter would startle her sensibility and force her to realize that she was risking losing my affection.

I didn't want any errors in my letter, so I gave it to my mom to read. When she finished the letter, she paused for a moment. Finally she said, "It's a nice letter. But are you sure you want to give it to Toni? Why don't you wait a couple of days and see how you feel about it?"

I could suddenly sense some of my cocksureness drain away. As she handed me the letter, she added, "By the way, what if she chooses Howard?" The possibility had never crossed my mind. Her question cooled my enthusiasm for forcing Toni to make a choice, and it opened the door for self-doubt to creep in.

As I got up to leave, I wadded up the letter and dropped it into the wastebasket.

I never did write to Toni. Things just took their natural path, and we drifted apart before the year was over.

Years later, when I was well into middle age, Mom turned over to me the family archives. Among the documents and photos was a frayed and wrinkled piece of paper that looked like it must have been folded and refolded many times. It was my letter to Toni. Mom had held onto it through several moves over the last fifty years.

When I reread the letter, I was struck by how simple and direct it was. I guess, in looking back, childhood always looks like that: simple and direct. At least the choices do.

Life After Youth

The young heroes of writer Joseph Conrad's stories are invariably brought to a crisis, which, if they survive, will bring them into manhood. They will have "crossed over" from youth.

I am a man, but somehow I got here without the crisis. Furthermore, I don't remember the moment of crossover either.

I do remember little adventures, like in the fourth grade, sneaking off with Sammy Nichols who lived in the same apartment complex as we did. We'd go off to the local market, supposedly to buy cigarettes for our parents. Then we'd take them behind the apartments by the woods and smoke (or try to smoke) one or two a piece. By the end of fifth grade I'm sure I tried every cigarette brand the market carried. Maybe it wasn't a fair trial because neither of us ever learned how to inhale without burning our throats and gagging. Anyway, smoking was a big disappointment.

Adults showed us that smoking cigarettes was about the coolest thing a guy could do. On the TV they always said things like, "Winstons taste good like a cigarette should," "Lucky Strike means fine tobacco," "I'd walk a mile for a Camel," and "Us Tarrington smokers would rather fight than switch." You get the picture. Come to think of it, our study hadn't been a total waste of time. For one thing, neither Sammy nor I ever became smokers, and for another, we had taken another step closer to adulthood.

In the seventh grade we discovered girls. We used to play Spin the Bottle at parties in the storage rooms of the apartment complex. And I'm telling you, the kissing was hot and heavy. We kissed with passion, for seventh graders. After a session of Spin the Bottle, Sammy and I felt a strange stirring in our adolescent bodies. We knew we were on our way.

In high school and college making out led to serious romances. Your grades went down, even as your spirit went up. Love. It was a euphoric, agonizing time that often led to marriage, which was surely an adult institution.

Then you got out of college. A few years passed by, and you were in suburbia with two and a half kids. That's when you started feeling like you'd missed something. You were beginning to wonder where your youth had gone. That feeling of immortality, the freedom from responsibilities, mortgages, bills, braces? So this was adulthood!

You went to class reunions and spent the evening reminiscing about the good old days in high school.

Then you hit your forties and began to try to recreate yourself. You're in the gym, you're counting calories, you're checking your cholesterol. You're doing all that you can do to recapture your youth.

By your fifties, it's becoming clear this is a battle you're not going to win. Things have started to sag that never used to. Your skin doesn't fit as tight as it once did. Muscles that used to be dependable are suddenly rebelling. You turn flabby despite your best efforts. Your biggest wish is that you'd bought stock in Max Factor or Revlon when you could have, or in some company that discovers the cure for cellulite.

Movements your body used to make willingly it now does reluctantly, if at all. And you can't help comparing it to the way it was when you were young.

This story could get depressing if I don't watch it. Personally, I have ambivalent feelings about youth. It looks great in retrospect. Especially when you compare it to what may be waiting ahead.

Indoctrination: Once Was Enough

I got myself indoctrinated once. I have to admit, I asked for it. I was just short of my 21st birthday, living in the eternal drizzle of Seattle. Barely carrying a 2-point in my third year of college, I was deeply depressed, waiting for something to come along that I could grab hold of and pull myself out of the mire.

It was 1958. In those days young men over the age of 18 were obligated to serve in some branch of the military for a three or four year hitch. Needing a drastic change, I joined the Marines.

The Marines didn't use the word "indoctrination," they called it "training" or "conditioning". To take a soft civilian like me, who had never fired a shot in anger, and turn him into a soldier who could put a bullet in a man's head at 500 yards, and feel good about it, took training. We were proud to be called "trained killers." In this killing, which thank God I never had to do, we were trained to see our enemies not as people but as "gooks" or "slopes." Make them less human than ourselves.

In my last week of combat training, we were in a war game in the boondocks of Camp Pendleton. We were walking through a field of tall weeds. The enemy was supposed to be out there ready to either ambush us or pick us off one at a time from sniper positions. As we advanced, every ten yards or so a target would pop up out of the weeds. If we got a few rounds into it fast enough, it would sink back down into the weeds, dead! If we were not quick enough, then *we* were "dead." What struck me during this exercise was that all of the targets were wornout little yellow men with round spectacles and buckteeth. This was the stereotypical Japanese soldier of the Second World War, which had ended thirteen years earlier. Although the little yellow men represented a country that was now our ally, they were still Japs to the Marines. It's much easier to shoot a Jap than a Japanese.

A few months later we went to Korea on an assignment. The Korean conflict had been over for six years. Our army had settled in among our South Korean allies, whom our soldiers referred to as gooks or slopes, and treated them as second-class citizens in their own country. Some soldiers were openly hostile. They drove through the villages at high speeds. If a slope got accidentally knocked into a ditch by a two and a half ton truck, it wasn't the Army's fault, the old lady should have been more careful. Discussing this kind of bigotry in the barracks doesn't make you popular. It makes people think who don't want to.

After we got back from Korea, I volunteered for a

four-month assignment on Okinawa. One night when I was feeling lonely and philosophical, I wrote a letter to my buddies back in Hawaii. I liked the Okinawans, and I liked the Japanese. In the letter I championed the equality of all men, all colors. I was a young man learning things about myself, and I wanted to share it all.

I wrote about my disgust with how we treated the Koreans, and how we saw the Okinawans as lowly hired help, and the Japanese as nothing better. I wrote something about loving my fellow man, and that included my buddies back in Hawaii.

A few months later I was back with my outfit and headed for Taiwan on a troop transport. We were out of sight of land somewhere in the South China Sea. Two sergeants called me over to the rail. They said they had read the letter I wrote from Okinawa (my friend had posted it on the bulletin board). These two buck sergeants, one a supply clerk and the other a tall, bent, bony bastard who terrorized the members of his squad, calmly told me they were thinking about throwing me overboard. They said they didn't want any faggoty college boys around them, talking about brotherly love.

I was nonplussed. I didn't know what to say. That these two cretins had read the letter in the first place was a total shock to me. I didn't want to defend myself. And I certainly didn't want to explain myself or excuse what I'd written. Luckily there were a few other guys on deck, including a couple of buddies. Otherwise, I think there would have been a man overboard, with no alarm sounded. Such things have happened before. From that day on until I got out, I watched my back.

A few months later I was a short timer. That's a guy with less than thirty days to go on his enlistment. There was some scuttle about whether or not to allow me to re-enlist, this because of my "attitude." I had no intention of re-enlisting, but the rumor galled me. I had a perfect record, a good conduct medal, and was promoted three times, which was the maximum for a three-year hitch. The word was that I wasn't gung ho enough to stay in the Corps. They were right. My training had worn off.

I was free to think for myself, but I'll give the Corps credit where it's due. They had created in me a sense of self-reliance, and they had also given me the self-discipline I had been sorely lacking. I was never successfully indoctrinated again. A few people tried, but they didn't get far. I owe that to the Corps.

Semper Fi.

Mr. Macho

I was pretty macho in my day, my day being before I got married. I didn't tie the knot until I was thirty-nine. After all those years of bachelorhood, I had my macho image well honed.

In the nine years before I met my wife, I had a full beard. While marking me as some kind of social rebel, that beard was also great to hide behind whenever I felt threatened, especially by a woman. Feminism was rampant at the time, and I got a perverse satisfaction from doing my best to slow its progress.

I remember one time in a high school class I was team-teaching with my best friend, Ray. We were showing a film about a Greek family that was desperately trying to hold on to their small candy store in a neighborhood that was being torn down around them. They were the victims of crooked politicians and urban renewal. Finally, they lost the battle and were forced out of their store and the apartment where they had lived for over forty years.

Tough ass that I was, the minute the film was over, I jumped in with my unsolicited critique, which, as usual, was mainly negative. Thinking I would get support from some of the students, I waited for their response. Finally, one girl said, "You've just ruined that movie for the rest of us. I thought it was a beautiful story about the heroism of one family."

"But it was sappy," I said, mustering some false bravado.

"It was sappy for you," she said, "because it dealt with human emotions, and that always makes you nervous and defensive. Then you retreat into your Mr. Macho routine."

Oh, crap! I thought. Here it goes again. Ray and I had fifty of the brightest, most creative kids in the school for two hours a day, five days a week. At that time, teachers were supposed to make their classes "relevant" to the students' lives. We were on a first-name basis with the students, and they took every advantage of the situation, especially the group of budding feminists who hung out together. They had decided that their role in life was to save me from myself, as they put it, to open me up. They wanted to broaden my experience and challenge what they called my macho bullshit. These seventeen-year-olds were already well versed in the principles of feminism.

As I remember the feminist movement, it was all about simultaneous orgasms and erotic zones. It had a period of furry legs and bristling pits. It also was a time when American men were having midlife crises of their own. I could feel the erosion of my manhood, and the more confused it got, the more I machoed.

Don't get me wrong. I fully agreed that women were getting a raw deal in the job market. I agreed that they deserved the same salaries that a man got for the same job. The problem was that in giving them credit for one part of their agenda, you were expected to support them in the rest. I didn't even know what the rest was. To them, you were either with 'em or against 'em. And if you were against them you'd get labeled a male chauvinist pig. (OINK!)

About now comes into my life a young woman. She was a new teacher at the high school where I taught. She was a mix of traditional family values and four years of college, where she'd learned that women had put up with catering to men's whims and desires long enough. Why should a woman, for example, have to shave her legs to please men? Men don't shave their legs. The same for armpits. A silly custom created...to please men.

As the feminist movement was reaching its zenith in the middle seventies, I began to sense that my macho image wasn't working the way it used to. I was beginning to feel like an anachronism of some sort. What women wanted, they said, was vulnerability, not machismo. God! How many workshops did I sit through, how many hours did I spend in therapy trying to be vulnerable? Trying to get in touch with my feelings? How to express my child within? How to explore and express my feminine side? (I didn't even know I had one.)

Of course, I married the girl with the traditional

values and the feminist bent. That was twenty-six years ago. I'm not so macho anymore. It doesn't work with her or my two daughters.

I know where the mask is hanging, and I can still wear it in situations that bring up old fears. But I no longer feel a kinship with the Marlboro Man. He's still out there, riding the range, in all kinds of weather, with his cowboy buddies. It's really kind of sad. There are no women in his life, so he'll never know the joys of being vulnerable. He had his chance.

With a little compromise, he could have been just the thing the American Woman has always longed for: a cowboy in touch with his feelings.

The Autumn of My Life

Fall is here and there's nothing I can do about it. I tried my best to hold it off, but it's bigger than I am. You know, first the air starts to get a little brisk, and the days get shorter. Then your mood sinks and you go to bed earlier. That's Fall.

The season's not called Fall for nothing. My deck, for example, is covered with cracked and crinkled buckeye leaves. My dog's coat is growing longer because she's ready for the colder weather. And my mood, as my wife will attest, is sinking fast.

The word "Autumn" softens things a bit. It's certainly more romantic than the word "Fall". The trees turning saffron yellow across the river. The handsome couple in the cardigan sweaters walking through a mapled canyon, with their golden retriever romping at their side. The exotic scent of bay leaves in the air. The mergansers fishing for minnows that will never make it to the sea. The Great Blue Herons waiting patiently for the frog eggs to turn to tadpoles. I see all that.

Still, I do not like Fall.

Winter I can handle. It has a purpose, I can live with it. Spring is a happy time, a rebirth, a resurrection, a renewal of the spirit. I like Spring. Summer is full of childhood memories. Most of a kid's best times are in the summer. It's exciting, it's full of adventures, and it has light. You can stay outside and play kick-the-can till nine o'clock. Or you can just sit and talk, and feel the warmth. Then, just as you have fully settled into Summer, along comes Fall.

When I think about it, I guess Fall reminds me of my mortality. I have seen myself grow, bud, and blossom. And, to follow the metaphor, I have seen my leaves change color. But unlike me, the buckeye doesn't die and cease to be. In its dormancy, it rests. And in the Spring, like the Christ, it rises from the dead and blooms anew.

Maybe this Fall I'll learn to cherish what lies before me. After all, this is the Autumn of my life, and unlike the buckeye, I won't be going 'round again.

nearest and dearest...

Out at Second

When I was a little kid, my mother set up a kind of code between us. She told me, that if I had done something bad, to tell her the truth and I wouldn't get spanked. If I got into trouble and I told her before she heard it from somebody else, I'd be the better for it.

The first time I tested her on this agreement, I was three. I used to watch my dad sharpen the big carving knife by stroking it back and forth, up and down against one of those long knife sharpeners. Dad would hold the sharpener in one hand and the knife in the other, sort of like stropping a razor.

Unfortunately, I didn't pay enough attention to Dad's stropping technique. I knew Mom liked her knives to be really sharp, so the next day I took her knives out of the lined box she kept them in and I banged the blades together. It looked to me like what Dad did. But instead of making the knives sharper, it gave them all serrated edges.

Later that afternoon Mom called me into the

kitchen. She was holding one of the knives I'd sharpened.

"Did you do this?" she asked.

"Yes," I answered proudly. But I noticed that Mom didn't look as delighted as I thought she would.

"Why?" she asked.

"I saw Daddy do it," I said.

She looked at me in total exasperation. After telling me what I had done to her knives, and telling me to never go near them again, she said, "Now go on out and play. And stay out of trouble." I had told the truth, and saved my fanny.

The next time I tested Mom was one morning after I had watched Dad trim his eyebrows, which tended to get bushy. After he went to work, I thought I should do what Dad did. Once again I hadn't watched as closely as I should have.

"Good grief!" Mom said when she saw me. "What have you done to your eyes?" When she asked me again what happened, I told her the truth. "I trimmed them," I said.

"Trimmed?" she replied. "You've cut off your eyelashes! You are all eyeballs." Then she let out a kind of sigh, mumbled something I couldn't hear, and went into the other room. Once again the truth had saved me. But it wasn't doing much for Mom.

I remember one time the truth didn't work. I was three and we were visiting Grandma and Grandpa in Porterville. I went next door to play with the neighbor boy. He and I went out in the field behind his house, made a sort of fort in the tall grass, and spent some time examining our body parts. An hour later I went into the house and was walking into the living room, when suddenly Grandma lurched out of her chair and grabbed me by the cheek.

"What have you been doing, you nasty little boy?"

"Nothing," I said. My cheek was really hurting and I started to cry.

"Don't lie to me. The straps on your overalls are crossed in the back. They weren't when you went out. You've had your pants off!"

In the face of my guilt and embarrassment, I went silent. For my insolence, I was sent to bed hours before my bedtime.

I was puzzled. I had lied to Grandma, I knew that. But if I'd told the truth, the truth being that I'd rather be playing Pee-Pee Touch with the kid next door than sitting in a room full of adults, I don't think the truth would have worked so well.

When I got a few years older, I discovered that, despite my best intentions, sometimes the truth could get me into trouble. When I was in high school playing baseball, in one game I hit a shot to right field hard enough to make me try to stretch it into a double. I slid into second base a hair after the second baseman laid tag on me. It was a hard call for the umpire. For one thing, he was in the wrong position to see the tag. For another, my slide kicked up a lot of dust.

Both the second baseman and I were in a heap on the ground. The ump couldn't make the call. So he walked over to us and said, "I couldn't see the play, were you out or safe?" No umpire had ever asked me that before. I guess I was caught off guard, I don't know, but I said I was out.

When I got back to the dugout, some of the players couldn't even look at me. A few of them had some remarks about what a dork I was, and how could anybody be that stupid. The coach was really miffed. "That was the dumbest thing I've ever seen. You never tell an ump you're out. That's his job, that's what he's paid for."

I didn't start the next day. The coach started a guy off the bench. Things were never the same between the coach and me. I guess I'd lost his respect, or he didn't trust me anymore. I don't know.

But I did learn a little bit more about truth. You have to be careful with it. You can't tell the truth all the time. Sometimes you have to lie a little. That is, if you want to stay in the game.

A Bird of Space

In my youth, I told a girl I loved her. She looked at me a moment, and said, "I don't know what that means. You'll have to show me." I was taken aback. I was sure she'd know what I meant. I was perplexed. It worked in all the movies.

Now, years later, I think I know what she was saying: love is an abstraction, like friendship or honor or courage. It means little until you give it shape or size or image. "Love" becomes more meaningful when taken as a verb: the act of loving. This is what that girl knew long ago. She was wise beyond her years.

Listen to this simple metaphor:

> *"Love is a bird of space*
> *that in a cage of words*
> *may indeed unfold its wings,*
> *but cannot fly."*

If you really want to keep love you have to let it go. A hard paradox to live with.

I don't know who wrote that poem. I don't know where it came from or whether I've got it right. But somehow it lodged itself in a dark corner of my mind and stayed there. Once in a while it comes forward and presents itself, without summons.

In my father's generation it was hard to talk of love at all. He could never say, "I love you" to anyone in the family. It was too intimate. I never heard my dad say, "I love you" to Mom. In my adult years I resented him for that. She was a woman who needed to hear those magic words, sometimes desperately. Instead of telling her himself, he'd buy the mushiest cards he could find for her birthday, Mother's Day, Easter, etc. He was a heavy supporter of Hallmark.

When he and Mom split up when I was in high school and Mom moved to L.A., he'd call her at night after several highballs and ask her to listen to some love song he'd picked out of his collection of musicals. Writing this right now I'm beginning to see him in a new light. But back then, I couldn't understand why he wouldn't put his generation aside and give her the words she wanted to hear.

And as for Mom, didn't she realize that he had found a way to use the lyrics, the voice of others, to say what he felt but couldn't say? His technique must have worked. She came back, and when she left him a few years later he wooed her back again. By then, he knew all of the lyrics by heart.

As for myself, after two years of therapy and another eight years in a men's group, I finally discovered that I really did have a father who loved me, although he'd never say it.

In the last part of his life (he died at 86) he worried about my finances. I sometimes resented his concern. I had quit teaching after seventeen years and couldn't find another job. He was probably worried about my mental health, too. I was pretty well into alcohol, hiding out in it, being ashamed in it, getting depressed and dispirited. Dad saw that.

He tried to give me things...a boat, cars, money, but I was "asserting my independence." It was about time. I was in my late forties, and Dad in his early eighties. I wouldn't accept the boat, I didn't accept the cars. The money was another matter. One day during a session, the therapist told me that I was, by refusing his gifts, denying my father a chance to love me. I countered with a glib, "He doesn't know how to love."

The therapist snapped back, "You just want love to look the way you want it to, to fit your picture of it."

"Doesn't everyone have their own idea about love?" I asked.

"Of course," he said, "but in your case your picture includes a kind of father you never had. And you'd better get this straight. He isn't going to change his personality, his being, just so he can fit into your picture."

The therapist was on to something. He wanted to drive it home. "Your father has been trying to express his love for you the only way he knows how, by giving you things, not words, not 'Son, I love you,' but 'Son, take the boat, I don't use it any more.' Or, 'Son, take the car off my hands. Yours is in pretty bad shape, come on over and pick this one up. It's not bad.'"

"That was love?" I asked.

"It's love, not the way you pictured it, but the only way he knows how to show you. You've been denying him that for years."

Dad no doubt had his picture, too. I had never really thought about it from his side. I knew I'd always wanted to have a father. I didn't know he wanted to have a son.

Big Boys Don't Kiss

We didn't touch in my family. It just wasn't done. I don't know whose fault it was, it just was. My dad told me he never saw his parents touch each other. Obviously they had to be together to raise the family, but never a display of touching, let alone hugs and kisses.

One time when I was a little boy, Mom and I went to the airport to pick up Dad who was coming home after a business trip. When he had come home from trips in the past, there was always a hug and a kiss for me. But this time when I went to kiss him on the cheek he turned from me. "Men don't kiss men," he said. "You're a big boy now and big boys don't kiss." "Can we hug?" I asked. "No, men don't hug either."

I've never forgotten that day. Something slipped in between me and my father, and it never slipped out again. When I got out of the service at the age of twenty-three, I went to stay with my folks for a few weeks. It was a Spartan existence on a mushroom farm that was not paying off. Dad was working a sixty-hour week, and he could not get out of the red. My mother was working for a dollar twenty-five an hour for some cheap drugstore. She came home tired and sullen, with booze on her breath. It was not a healthy scene, but I stuck around working with Dad for minimum wage, trying to raise mushrooms.

It was during this time that I appointed myself the savior of their marriage, which had already suffered some separations, one of which lasted over a year. They were held together by habit, not love. At least not the way I wanted love to look when I got married.

Mom was physically needy. She ached to touch and be touched. Except for a few times when he was in his cups, there was never an arm over Mom's shoulder, never a squeeze of her hand, not even a pat on the fanny. Actually, Dad liked to pat fannies, just not hers. He also became a boob checker. When we'd all go out to lunch together it had to be at one of Dad's favorite restaurants. He knew the waitresses and they knew him. If he'd been drinking they knew not to come too close to him when they were serving. Otherwise they'd have to explain to their husbands how they got the little pinch marks they had on their derriers.

How did Dad get away with this? For one thing, he was a big tipper. Furthermore, when he was sober he was a nice guy. The booze freed the letch in him. No, that's not quite right. It freed the guy who liked to play the letch, to act the part. Dad was not a sexual guy. I guess the waitresses knew he'd never follow through in any sexual way. They'd humor him with lines like, "Be a nice boy, now," or "God, you're such a kidder!" This routine went on into his eighties, and with Mom and my wife and our kids sitting there with us, it never got better.

As I said earlier, I decided to straighten Dad out and save the marriage, which was heading for a permanent break. You may say, "Hey, it was none of your business." What can I say? I was twenty-three.

I began to nag Dad about giving Mom some physical attention. He fought me off. In the meantime, Mom kept coming home half crocked. She and a lady clerk she worked with kept sipping vodka all day, until they were well on their way by four o'clock. She almost got fired, but her boss could never find anyone who would work for such lousy money, drive her own car on deliveries, and even buy her own gas.

Anyway, all my nagging went for naught. Dad never touched her. I'm embarrassed to say I never did either. In trying to straighten out Dad, I completely let myself off the hook. This sounds strange, but the needier she got, the more I pulled away. I knew what she wanted but I couldn't give it to her. It's humbling to have to admit to the old saw: "like father, like son."

I'd grown up with a series of dogs and cats of all varieties. Through the years we also had goats and chickens and geese, but by far first on Dad's list was ducks. I've raised a few ducks myself. One time I had a baby mallard named Dempsey who grew up to be quite a character. Dempsey was about as cute as a duck can get, and wonderfully affectionate.

At three days old, I took him over to my folks in Aptos to show him off. Dempsey's favorite activity was to sit on your shoulder and nibble on your ear while making these soft little peeping sounds. That's exactly what Dempsey did when I put him on Dad's lap. He went up the front of Dad's bathrobe, with a little boost, found his spot on Dad's shoulder, and began his nibbles and peeps. If Dempsey missed his target and stuck his beak in Dad's ear, Dad would giggle like a little boy and scold Dempsey: "Hey, duck, not too hard!" Dad acted like he was like a little kid transported back to Miles City, Montana, where his parents had a sheep ranch.

I know this will sound crazy, but suddenly I wanted to sit on Dad's shoulder and peep in his ear. But I know that men don't do that.

The Orchid

When I asked Ellen Seeberger to the prom, I never thought I had a chance. When she said yes, I was flabbergasted. I don't mean to imply that I was some sort of nerd. I was more of a know-it-all, desperate for attention. But the state of my sophomore psyche is not what I want to tell you about.

My best friend that year was Harold Swartz. He lived with his mother in a small apartment a few miles from our house. He was half a year older than me, had his driver's license, and spent most of his time working on an old car he inherited from an elderly aunt. He was rebuilding it from scratch, little by little. To pay for it he worked nights at the bowling alley.

Harold was old for his age. He was also very serious. We had become friends struggling through Latin in our freshman year. My dad trusted him completely. He let Harold teach me how to drive in my dad's cherry, 1951 cream-colored Buick convertible. Harold didn't drink, smoke, have tattoos, or drive crazy. Also, he had never been to a prom.

When I asked him if we could double date and use my dad's car, he paused for a moment, then he told me he knew a girl he'd like to ask. The girl turned out to be Allison Fox, a girl I knew in the eighth grade. She never excited me much. Straight A student, three inches taller than me, and serious. As the prom drew near, one evening my dad asked,

"What kind of corsage are you going to get for your date?"

"Corsage?" I said. "What's a corsage?" I had no idea. Like Harold, I'd never been to a prom either.

"Get her an orchid," Dad said. "Girls go nuts for orchids."

Since Dad obviously knew more about proms than I did, the next day I trotted off to the flower shop to order an orchid corsage.

"An orchid corsage? How nice. That'll be fourteen dollars plus tax." The clerk could tell by looking at me that fourteen dollars was a lot more than I had. What I had was five dollars and forty-two cents. "Well," she said, "when you get the money, come back."

When I told my dad that I was going to get Ellen a less expensive corsage, he laughed. "Son, you'll never get a girl with anything less than an orchid. Besides, she'll think you're cheap. It'll reflect on the family." He paused for a moment, then he added, "I'll give you the rest of the money."

I was beginning to feel that the orchid was more important to Dad than it was to me, but what could I say?

The night of the prom I went to the flower shop

and picked up the orchid corsage. It was big. If Ellen wore it pinned to the front of her dress, even on her shoulder, I was sure I'd smash it on the first dance. When Dad saw the orchid, his face lit up. "Now that's what I call a corsage," he said. "It'll knock her socks off!" I wasn't so sure.

Harold came over and we went off in the Buick to pick up our dates. "What's in the box?" he asked.

"Just a flower," I replied.

"Some flower," he said. "Is it still in the pot?"

"No, it's just sort of big. It's an orchid."

"Oh," he said. Then he fell quiet.

At the dance, we gave our dates their corsages, which were still in boxes from the florist. They went to the girls' room. When they came out, my date had a strange look on her face. She looked embarrassed. Next to her stood Allison, wearing a small white carnation on her wrist. Next to the orchid on Ellen's shoulder strap, the carnation looked dinky.

I felt like a fool. Why hadn't I realized that Harold wouldn't have the money to buy a big, showy corsage? And he didn't have a dad to buy it for him. How could I be such a jerk?

Thank God the band started to play. Gratefully, we all headed for the dance floor. Once we got into the music, things went pretty well. I never did crush the orchid, although it got a little wimpy by the end of the evening. Harold never mentioned the orchid again, and I was more than willing to let it go.

After the prom when I got home, Dad was still up. He asked me how my date liked her corsage. "Great, really great. Thanks, Dad."

"Glad to help," he said, and went to bed.

I learned something that night, although I wasn't aware of it at the time. I certainly couldn't have put it into words. But in remembering how I felt, something had gone wrong, and I didn't know how to make it right.

Years later I came to see the incident as a lesson telling me to start trusting myself, my own intuition. I had known the orchid was too big, just as I knew Harold couldn't afford one, and that he didn't have a dad to bail him out. As for my dad, he meant well. The orchid was something special to him. I never knew what.

The following year, Harold said he was so busy with school and his new job that he'd have to skip the prom this year. I drove myself to the prom. I took a girl I met in Biology. I bought her a mum.

Dad's Lost Ranch

When I graduated from college and became sophisticated, I decided that my father was a lot like Willie Loman. In case you don't recall the play, Willie Loman was the protagonist in Arthur Miller's *Death of a Salesman*. We met Willie at the end of his life, a life he had wasted trying to live up to the expectations of the American Dream.

My dad was much like Willie, the noticeable difference being that Willie was never cut out to be a salesman while my dad was a natural. Personally, I never liked sales, or the whole business world, for that matter. To me business was the reason a man spent the bulk of his time away from his family. That was how I felt at ten or eleven. I've mellowed some since then.

One day I asked Dad whether he had ever read *Babbit* by Sinclair Lewis. Babbit pursued the American Dream, especially the material side. He defined himself by what he owned. The only joy he found in life was in a fantasy he created to ease his loneliness.

Dad picked up on the implication faster than I thought he would. I was certain that he had never read anything that would cause him to examine his values. In answer to my question, he responded with a terse, "I'm not a Babbit." Thus my plan, which was to lead him into a discovery of how shallow he was, never got off the ground. And Babbit never came up again.

Any time I spent around my father was usually in the past. I guess we felt safer there. For years, Dad had been talking about getting the ranch back. The ranch was three hundred acres of live oaks and redwoods off the Old Freedom Highway. It was a magnificent piece of property, well cared for by its previous owner. There was a three-story main house where we lived, plus a cottage for the caretaker and a guesthouse for overnighters, usually those who drank too much to drive home.

Ironically, we only owned the ranch for about a year. Then something went wrong with Dad's business and he lost it all. I never really understood what happened. It had to do with bankers who were jealous of Dad and wanted to take over his company, which they did. That's how Dad told it. One day I came home from school and found unfamiliar cars parked everywhere. All our furniture was out on the lawn. There were price tags on everything. We were losing the ranch, and this was the first I knew of it.

After the sale, we packed a few things into the car and headed off to Seattle where Dad would manage a lumberyard for an old friend until we got enough money to get the ranch back. That was the plan.

A few years later, Dad had another business underway in Seattle and was doing well. Then one night it burned to the ground. It was under-insured and couldn't be rebuilt. The return to the ranch would have to wait.

Eleven years later, the Seattle adventure being over, we returned to Aptos to "get a fresh start," as Dad put it. We'd been gone for over ten years and had nothing to show for it. Dad was deeply in debt, fifty-seven years old, and had no prospects. He was down, but not quite out. Once, when Mom and Dad were arguing over some money problem, suddenly Dad banged the tabletop with his hand, stood up, and proclaimed, "I may be broke, but I'm not poor." The argument was over.

He refused all suggestions from former business associates that he take the easy way out and declare bankruptcy. "After all," they counseled, "what have you got to lose?" His reply was simple: "I'm not going out a failure. I plan to pay back all I owe."

I don't know whether he ever got it all paid back or not, but he did make peace with the IRS. And he was never bankrupt.

In the years that followed, we built the return of the ranch into a kind of mantra, magic words that carried their own truth regardless of the state of things in the outside world. We even began to ritualize the dream, although we didn't know it at the time.

I was in my late twenties living in Carmel Valley. Dad was sixty-eight. Whenever I drove over to Aptos, the ritual would begin. First, I'd check in with Mom.

She usually had little chores for me, like replacing a light bulb or fixing a faucet. After that Dad and I would take off to the village on some important errand he'd forgotten to do. Then we'd make the rounds of the local bars for an hour before returning home. It was in the bars where we developed the ritual. We already had our lines down pat, so we could play with the language on the surface, but we stuck to our theme: the return of the ranch.

Never once did I suggest that the dream of the ranch was just that. Not once did I remind him that he was flat broke, and that the IRS was interested in any property he might ever own. Never did I remind him of what he already knew: that the current owner of the ranch loved it and had no plans to sell.

When I quit drinking, the ritual fell apart. I suppose alcohol was the glue that kept it together all those years. Anyway, Dad and I stopped making the rounds. I'd reached a point where I couldn't recite my lines anymore. After a while, Dad dropped the subject of the ranch.

We spent the remaining years of his life talking trivia. Neither one of us had any knack for it. My visits to Aptos became awkward and uncomfortable. I even began to resent them.

Dad finally got some money together and bought a mobile home in a nice park near Aptos. He'd sit on his front porch with Mom, waiting for the cocktail hour to start. That's when he was at his best.

The cocktail hour eventually became a ritual. Every-one knew his part. All the subjects for discussion never got too far afield. It did what rituals are supposed to do: give people a sense of belonging to something bigger than themselves, that their lives have meaning.

I can still see Dad in his eighties, sitting in his favorite chair on the porch, surveying his garden, waving to a passerby, and saying, more to himself than anyone else, "Isn't this the life? Where else would you want to live?" Finally, Dad had all the ranch he needed.

Mahalo, Mama

I can still see her, flopping over on the sand, laughing at an off-color joke I told. We were on a week's vacation on the Big Island, my mother and I. I'd never seen her so full of life. Hawaii, as she would say, had been her dream for years, and now she was living it.

The next day we picked up the rental car and headed out to explore. After a few minutes, Mom reached into the glove box and got out the auto insurance contract to give it a quick read. Suddenly she said, "Oh, oh!"

"What?" I said.

"Look at this." She held up the contract so I could see it. In the margin, in big, bold, red letters, it warned, "Do not drive this vehicle in volcanic areas. Volcanic dust damages catalytic converters. Furthermore, this insurance does not cover 'acts of God'," by which, I guess, they meant hot lava.

"What do you think?" Mom asked.

"What the hell," I said. "We came to see the whole

island." We took a hit from the pint of vodka Mom carried in her purse, and headed for the volcanoes. There were signs along the way: "Watch for Volcanic Activity."

We made it almost to the top. We couldn't drive all the way to the Visitor's Center because the rest of the road was covered by a recent lava flow about six inches thick. It was still warm to the touch. Her new hip was hurting her, but she was determined to do everything. She walked the last hundred yards to the Visitor's Center between my arm and her cane.

The scene before us was starkly beautiful, like being on the surface of a black moon. It was otherworldly. As we stood on the platform looking out over the cooling lava flow, Mom said, "This must be the hand of God the car insurance guys warned us about. I wonder if they've ever been here."

The following morning, I decided to teach Mom to snorkel. We went to a beach that had a dock for swimming. She was game but embarrassed. She could swim but she was 67 and hadn't had a bathing suit on in years. "Decades," she said. She did now, and she was nervous. It turned out she had a right to be. Luckily, there were very few people around. I soon found out that teaching someone to snorkel, especially when it's the first time for both student and teacher, is like teaching someone to knot their necktie. Looks simple, has hazards.

Once we had our gear on, we stepped off the dock into the water. Mom sank about a foot below the surface, and came back up spitting and sputtering. Her mask had slid up to her forehead and was half full of water. For a second I thought she might drown. I panicked and jerked the snorkel out of her mouth so she could get a breath. Unfortunately her teeth came with it.

Following my inept instructions on how to snorkel, instead of merely putting her lips around the outer flange of the mouthpiece, she put the whole thing into her mouth and clamped down on it. We were in water well over our heads. If those teeth went down we were in deep trouble. But Mom's reaction was amazing. She snatched her teeth out of mid air. Swear to God! Then she turned around so I couldn't see her face and popped her dentures back where they belonged.

Back on the dock, when she had regained her composure, she said she'd like to try again. We were sitting there sipping the vodka when I suddenly thought what we must have looked like to anyone nearby. They'd probably think it was a case of elder abuse.

"What's so funny?" she asked. "How could I see Hawaii with no teeth?"

We spent the rest of the day lying on the beach reading. We snorkeled again the next day in shallow water with more success. And Mom left her teeth in the car.

Back home, on Halloweens she was at her best. Into her eighties, she'd dress up like a witch with this big, black hat, and sit on the front porch and give out candy. The kids were supposed to come up on the porch so she could see their costumes. Then they got the candy. She was so scary, some of the kids never made it to the porch. Somehow, she'd see they got their candy anyway. She used to say it was her favorite role: "It's fun being a witch," she said, "and I was born for it."

Mom cooked the basics. So much that I still don't know what to order off a menu at restaurants more pricey than Burger King. Mom had mastered the art of making goop. Goop, for those unfamiliar with the more esoteric dishes in American cuisine, is hamburger, macaroni, and any vegetable that came out of a can. I loved goop. I grew healthy and round on it.

If the recipe for goop encourages you to broaden your culinary repertoire, consider another of Mom's triumphs, Tomato Soup Cake. Flour, eggs, walnuts, Crisco, chocolate, more Crisco, and one can of tomato soup. Once baked, swath it in chocolate frosting about a half an inch thick. This, as Joseph Campbell said, is bliss.

Mom turned 97 this year. Although she doesn't make goop anymore, she can still smell the flowers of Hawaii.

What I Really Want to Say

Let sleeping dogs lie, the old saying goes. If it ain't broke, don't fix it. Leave things be. Don't rock the boat. And for Christ's sake, don't open that can of worms. Having pondered each of these old saws, which undoubtedly come from the collective wisdom of people who never took their own advice, I have decided to ignore them. Take the risk, and place my fledgling faith in the lap of love.

The assignment this week is not without its hazards. It reads, "What I Really Want To Say." You can say whatever you want to whomever you want. I'm writing to my wife.

Marikay, I love being married to you. I am a fortunate man, and although our communication is a strong part of our union, I feel the need to put something out there that you already know. But I need to put it into words.

For the past seventeen years we have been living with a stranger in the house. He was quiet when he first arrived. I hardly noticed him at all. But in the past couple of years he has become increasingly obnoxious and abusive. It reminds me of the old Monty Woolley movie, "The Man Who Came To Dinner." He never went home. The film is a comedy and played for laughs. In our case, the humor is hard to come by. We'll have to seek it out and make the most of it when it comes our way. Of course, our uninvited visitor is PD, Parkinson's Disease.

What's happening in our marriage is not unusual when a chronic disease decides to move in. The Parkinson's journals are full of articles on the subject. As the disease progresses and demands more attention from the person with PD, the healthy partner takes on more and more of the responsibilities that used to be shared. The caregiver (I hate the word!) has the best of intentions. But, and here's the irony, unless the person with PD is well centered and sure of himself, he may see her offers to help as further proof that he's losing it. He's no longer who he was. And that can add to his anger about what's happening to him.

If I allow myself to spend much time in the future creating "what if" stories about my health, I'll have myself in diapers by the end of the week.

I appreciate the ways you watch over me. I know you sometimes resent it, especially when I'm less than cooperative. Who wouldn't resent it? This is not what you signed on for. If I leave my cane in the car or refuse to use my walking stick, which helps my balance, it's simply my stubborn denial. If I sit there with my mouth open (becoming a mouth breather like John Elway) and look like a dying Buddha, remind me to shut it. I'm angry with my body, I call it names from the dark side of my vocabulary. I use verbal abuse on inanimate objects around the house that won't cooperate with me the way they used to. But enough of that.

I remember the time in my macho days, before we got married, when I asked you if you'd make it across the desert with me. When things got rough, and we were low on water, would you drop out on me? Or would you knuckle down and finish the trek? Would you be by my side when we reached the other side?

I know, it sounds like the plot for a John Wayne movie. But that was twenty-seven years ago and that's where I was at the time. You didn't like the metaphor. In fact, it angered you.

It does look pretty corny, and maybe even offensive from here. But how was I to know that twenty-seven years later, you'd be driving the wagon?

Evynn's Journey: Chapter One

My daughter Evynn left for college this morning.
I miss her already.

I'm not ready for this passage, although I admit
there have been times when I could have paid her to
go early. I'm sure she felt the same about me.

It's a case of parental ambivalence: part of me wants
her to get out there and take it on, whatever the "it" is.
Another part of me says, "Wait, not yet, she's not
ready." The girl knows nothing about housework. Her
roommates will hate her. She can't cook, she thinks pop-
ping a frozen waffle into the microwave is a culinary event.
She hangs her clothes on the floor. She'll perish out there.

That's the part of me who fears I haven't done
enough. It says I'm not the father I thought I'd be. We
didn't take long walks along the river, holding hands,
sharing her dreams for the future. We didn't stroll
through the park with our Golden Retriever while
discussing the subtle changes in the season. We didn't
share the intimate things that fathers and daughters

talk about on T.V. She never came to me for advice. That's not to say I never gave her any. As for teaching her to accept responsibilities, I wish I had spent more time there, even though my lectures were usually ignored. My best efforts to set her straight on the various aspects of life fell on deaf ears.

So why do I miss her? Mainly because she is life in abundance. She is ready to take on the world. It's all but impossible to argue her out of her position once it's fixed. The central theme of her argument is fairness. As a parent, that one line of defense can send you down some sticky roads.

Her mother and I have been telling her for years, only half jokingly, that she'd make a great judge. There would be no shades of gray in her courtroom. Her trials would be quick and fair. She could set the legal system back on track.

At least my attempts to prepare her for adulthood did one thing that may do her well in later life. I helped her build tight, rational appeals and denials. Once she has established her position on any issue, get ready for a challenge. No matter how good your arguments, she'll come back at you so many times that your defenses will crack from the sheer frustration of trying to defend them. After the cracks comes the cave-in.

What would save her courtroom from being dull is her sense of humor. There is one moment in her childhood I will always remember. One day when she was about five I came into the kitchen and found a large bag of potato chips on the table. There were little bits of chips everywhere. I called out to Evynn sitting in the next room, "Good grief, what happened?" There was no reply. I said, a little more forcefully, "Come in here, please."

Reluctantly she slowly poked her head through the doorway. "What?" she said.

"What?" I echoed. "What's all this mess?"

"I just did what it says," she replied.

"Says where?" I asked.

"Right there on the bag. See?"

On the potato chip bag in big bold letters were two words: "ONE POUND."

"That's what I gave it," she said. You'd be amazed what one good pound by a five-year old can do for a bag of potato chips.

I Had to Learn to Celebrate

I'd like to go around again. I missed a lot.

My family didn't do celebrations, not that I recall. As a result, I never knew what to do at events like weddings and anniversaries. My education regarding social functions was sadly lacking. I didn't know that at the time. My wife informed me after we were married.

Luckily for me, I married a woman who had a strong sense of family and knew how, as well as what, to celebrate. She's been the one to see that we weren't abandoned by our friends and relatives. I was ignorant of our celebratory customs.

I never knew what to take to weddings. When a female ex-student of mine invited me to her wedding, I wracked my brain for what would be an appropriate gift. Her future mother-in-law was one of the most domineering women I've ever met. Feeling that the bride would need all the help she could get, I gave her a bullwhip. It was a good piece of work, made of braided leather. It made more sense than another toaster. Unfortunately, the marriage didn't last. I guess the bride never got the hang of the whip.

When my next-door neighbors got married, I searched for a present that could add to the longevity of their union. I'd known the bride for a long time. She used to wander when the guy she married was away on business trips so I finally settled on silver and leather horse hobbles. The bride didn't see the humor in it. That marriage didn't make it either.

At one wedding I gave a couple a classy handcrafted metal steak plate. The bride, another former student, confronted me on the street a few months later and said she found my present rather odd. Was something lost, or did I plan on her eating alone for the rest of her life? I could see that she was a little miffed when she said good-bye and walked off. It wasn't until months later than I found out that steak plates come in sets. Nobody gives only one.

We never went to funerals either. I understand that, at least in California, funerals are becoming more about celebrating a person's life rather than his death. You know, going out in a positive way. They've brought this to an art form in New Orleans in the black community, where a jazz band will play you all the way to the grave. People dance and sing the sadness away along the route.

My dad's idea of a celebration was someone springing for another round at the Red Rooster. Dad was an alcoholic, but a good man. I remember his various attempts to moderate his drinking throughout his adult life. Like most serious drinkers trying to get some control over their lives, he'd make resolutions that he truly meant to keep. One of those, which came around about once a year, went like this: "From now on, I'll only drink at celebrations." For Dad, celebrations were things like hearing the dentist say, "Good news, no cavities," or finally getting that damn gopher that was driving him nuts, or finding a ten spot on the pavement with no one around. A real drinker could celebrate a Roufus Towhee on the birdfeeder.

My wife's family did celebrations. They looked forward to them. They loved being with old friends. There was some drinking, but next to my family, they were lightweights. Because of them, slowly I began to feel almost comfortable in family gatherings. I'm still working on it.

A friend of mine once said the real joy of celebrations is to celebrate yourself. At first it sounded like a cliché from some pop guru from the '60's. But it goes further back than that. It rings true throughout the ages. To come to see yourself clearly; to assess and accept who you are; to find your place in the great scheme of things; to glory in the discovery of your own worth—this is the celebration.

I hear Walt Whitman singing the song of himself. In the "Song of the Open Road" he says, "I am better, larger, than I thought. I did not know I had half so much goodness." That's worth celebrating — the discovery of goodness in the journey, and kindess in us all.

Tree Frog
by Alyse LeValley, at age 19

He tried to write,
more than tried, did.
He loves the spilling of words
and the batter they become.
My father spent a year
with a typewriter and me,
a child drawing mustaches on my face
to look like him.

My father's eyes mischievously ignite sometimes
and I have his eyes,
restful, crescent moons in our faces
when we smile,
or turn to sarcasm
another inheritance,
along with words and pen mustaches.

At that age
my mother picked my clothes,
if I felt like wearing any.

At that age
I usually didn't,
neighbors laughed at my
dirt-covered nakedness.
At that age
exploring desert dry rivers
was landing on the moon,
and finding crusts of frogs.

When I was at that age,
he was writing.
Typing separate keys,
square fingers moving slowly.
But my father didn't have anything to say.

We used to mow the lawn.
He guided a hand-pushed mower.
I stood on the bar
watched the blades spinning under me,
my legs splattered with grass shreds.
My mother yelled that I'd lose a toe,
but he whispered that I didn't need them all anyway.

The contentment of riding in the clippings;
climbing onto that pile of fresh grass,
inside the womb of the blue wheelbarrow,
and taking a rolling bath,
splashing grass all down the street
as my father pushed me.

I came home green,
blond hair streaked with grass,
skin a fresh grass papier-maché;
and I pretended like I hadn't
ridden the lawn mower.
It was a cluefully green secret.
My father wrote for a year,
between the times
when I wanted to ride the mower,
or go exploring,
or build a doghouse,
or steal fruit from the neighbors' trees.
He wrote,
and the words never eluded him,
the beauty never escaped him,
but the point, the purpose,
the crux of all great stories…
well it dangles somewhere above our lawn, I guess.

He was never bitter,
as some unrealized dreamers are.
He just kept using words up,
looking for meanings.

My father once put a tree frog in my cereal,
right in the bowl with the milk.
I sat down on my dictionary booster,
and found round toes swimming in my cheerios,
like an old Esther Williams movie,
with a boggle-eyed star.

I did not scream, but my dinosaur eyes scrunched up,
almost as much as his,
as he laughed and pretended
it had jumped in the window.

I have all these pieces of my father:
his stories, his eyes, his humor, his love of word.
And I wonder sometimes
about purpose,
and whether I will find what he did not.

Thanks for coming along.
It makes the wait worthwhile.